CX-PRO
BEYOND THE BASICS

CX-PRO

BEYOND THE BASICS

Advanced Insights for Customer Experience Professionals

Edited by Karl Sharicz

PALMETTO
PUBLISHING
Charleston, SC
www.PalmettoPublishing.com

Paperback ISBN: 979-8-8229-5271-3
eBook ISBN: 979-8-8229-5272-0

Contents

Foreword

By Ken Peterson

Over the past four years I have worked closely with Karl Sharicz on a variety of Customer Experience initiatives. Our collective expertise in this space would likely require volumes of books to adequately represent our insights into Customer Experience operations and creating environments for operational excellence with nearly every industry.

At QuestionPro, we require every Customer Experience employee to attend the CX-PRO training to help them understand all the key aspects of Customer Experience management and workflows. From our sales teams to our client success representatives and even our product teams have a richer appreciation for the nuanced needs of both our QuestionPro clients along with what their customers demand from the research measurement, which goes beyond just a score. In addition to our employees, every one of our clients is offered an opportunity to participate in the CX-PRO training to get CX-PRO certification which mutually benefits all those involved in implementation by having a common understanding and set of definitions in the goals we are striving to achieve.

"CX-PRO: A Practical Guide for the New Customer Experience Manager" provides the initial groundwork for learning about Customer Experience practices and it wonderfully complements the CX-PRO training course while being a terrific guide for practitioners to reference during their day-to-day challenges. In *"Beyond the Basics,"* Karl is bringing experts with, cumulatively, centuries of experience in Customer Experience to provide additional advice and processes that will take programs to the next level.

Moving beyond building a Customer Experience program with a software platform, "Beyond the Basics" takes a detailed look at the role of the Frontline and C-Suite, creating compelling discussions and narratives to internally sell the success of the program, the role of emerging technologies—such as Generative AI—in Customer Experience and so much more. It goes beyond data analysis and gets into the importance of "job-to-be-done," which is why I was delighted to write the chapter about using Customer Experience to act.

You will find the stories from the authors' collective experiences to provide a wealth of information to make any CX practitioner successful and to continually hone their skills within the Customer Experience space.

Kenneth Peterson
President, QuestionPro CX

Introduction—Crafting Experiences, Shaping Futures

Karl Sharicz, EdM, CX-PRO

> *"The customer tells us how to stay in business, it's best that we listen."*
>
> **Pamela Nelson**

Welcome to the second CX-PRO book series where we build upon what was presented within the first book published in August 2023—*CX-PRO: A Practical Guide for the New Customer Experience Manager*—and expand upon some of the key topics of customer experience management (CXM) in a manner that helps lead us beyond the basics and into the more nuanced approaches and best practices of Customer Experience (CX). As today's business is a vast landscape described below by many interconnected factors, we must consider CX within that context to guide and help us successfully navigate that vastness.

1. **Globalization:** Advances in technology and transportation have facilitated the seamless flow of goods, services, and information across borders. This interconnectedness has expanded the reach of businesses, allowing them to operate on a global scale and tap into diverse markets.

2. **Technological Advancements:** The rapid pace of technological innovation has revolutionized every aspect of business operations. From automation and artificial intelligence to data analytics and digital communication platforms, technology has enabled businesses to streamline processes, enhance efficiency, and unlock new opportunities for growth.

3. **Market Diversity:** The modern marketplace is incredibly diverse, encompassing a wide array of industries, sectors, and niches. This diversity creates opportunities for specialization and differentiation, allowing businesses to cater to unique customer needs and preferences.

4. **Consumer Empowerment:** In today's digital age, consumers have unprecedented access to information, enabling them to make informed choices and exert greater influence over businesses. Their expectations for personalized experiences, exceptional service, and ethical business practices have reshaped the competitive landscape and compelled companies to prioritize customer-centricity.

5. **Entrepreneurial Spirit:** The barriers to entry for starting a business have lowered significantly, thanks to the proliferation of online platforms, crowdfunding, and supportive ecosystems for start-ups. This has led to a surge in entrepreneurial activity, fostering innovation and driving competition across industries.

6. **Regulatory Environment**: Businesses operate within a complex web of regulations and compliance standards that vary across regions and industries. Navigating this regulatory landscape requires careful attention to legal obligations, ethical considerations, and risk management practices.

7. **Economic Interdependence**: Economic interdependence is a hallmark of the modern business landscape, with companies relying on intricate networks of suppliers, partners, and stakeholders to sustain their operations. This interconnectivity introduces both opportunities for collaboration and vulnerabilities to systemic risks.

Given this vast landscape of modern business, one principle stands paramount above all and that is Customer Experience. It's the heartbeat of every successful enterprise, the North Star guiding decisions, and the thread that weaves together brand loyalty and sustainable growth. In this book you are reading, welcome to a journey through the multifaceted world of customer experience management—a journey articulated by sixteen diverse and inimitable voices, each illuminating a unique facet of this dynamic discipline.

At the helm of organizational strategy, we begin with "Aligning CX With the C-Suite." Here, **Patty Soltis** delves into the pivotal role of executive leadership in championing customer-centricity, underscoring the imperative of aligning organizational goals with the pursuit of exceptional customer experiences.

The journey transcends the boardroom, descending to the frontlines where the essence of CX unfolds. **Scott Gilbey** leads us on a journey toward "CX From a Frontline Perspective" and beckons us to see through the eyes of those directly engaging with customers, recognizing their pivotal role in shaping perceptions and forging enduring relationships.

Nurturing a cadre of proficient CX professionals is the cornerstone of sustainable success. In "Building Strong CX Professionals—Coaching, Mentoring, Self-care, and Community" **Jerry Seufert** illuminates a comprehensive approach required to cultivate empathetic, skilled, and resilient individuals poised to navigate the complexities of customer-centric environments in a caring and considerate manner.

As we traverse the landscape of customer service, **Alex Mead** demonstrates the value behind "Elevating the Customer Service Experience (CSX)" and **Jim Bass** shows us just how "The Net Promoter System (NPS) Done Right," when executed in the way it was originally developed, will unveil the intricacies of transforming interactions into memorable experiences and to harness customer feedback as a catalyst for growth.

The quest for excellence demands meticulous measurement and analysis of contextual data. **Gary David**, in his chapter on "Data Inventories for Better Experiences," underscores the significance of data-driven insights in refining strategies and optimizing touchpoints.

Beyond the numbers, lies the power of narrative. **Judy Bloch**, in "The Art & Science of CX Storytelling," explores the art of crafting immersive narratives that resonate with audiences, fostering emotional connections and brand allegiance.

In the ever-evolving digital landscape, **Marc Mandel** leads us into the topic of "The Emerging Role and Importance of AI in Managing the Customer Experience" and beckons us to embrace innovation, carefully leveraging artificial intelligence to enhance personalization and streamline operations.

Amidst the tumult of change, the CX professional emerges as a beacon of trust and guidance. "The CX Professional as a Trusted Guide" by **Mark Slatin** underscores the pivotal role of authenticity and integrity in fostering meaningful relationships with both organizations leaders and customers.

But knowledge alone is insufficient without action. **Ken Peterson**, in his chapter on "Using CX to Act," helps to propel us towards proactive engagement by listening to customers and empowering our organizations to act upon feedback, anticipate customer's future needs, and deliver exemplary service.

Professional growth is not solitary; it thrives within networks of collaboration and mentorship. "Networking and Professional Advancement" by **Greg Melia** advocates for the cultivation of vibrant communities, where knowledge-sharing and support amongst peers catalyze collective progress.

Grounded in the principles of human-centered design, **Eckhart Boehme** enlightens us through his chapter on "Customer Progress Design (jobs-to-be-done)" and underscores the importance of understanding customers' primary motivations and aspirations in crafting tailored experiences.

In the pursuit of excellence, quality reigns supreme. **Alec Dalton** takes us on a journey through his chapter on "A Quality Approach to CX Management" and advocates for a relentless commitment to excellence, where every interaction embodies the ethos of superior service.

Amidst the digital cacophony, "Understanding the Human Element in CX" by **Mark Borst** reminds us of the enduring power of the human connection, urging organizations to infuse empathy and authenticity into every interaction.

Within the corridors of every organization lie untapped reservoirs of insight—its employees. "Leveraging Employee Insights to Drive CX" by **Rich Dorfman** celebrates the transformative potential of internal perspectives, harnessing employee feedback and engagement as a catalyst for innovation.

Our journey culminates in the final chapter by **Laurie Gray** entitled "Customer Experience Career Paths," where she explores the myriad avenues for professional growth and fulfillment within the vibrant ecosystem of the customer experience management discipline.

Individually, these chapters offer profound insights into the nuances of customer experience. Collectively, they form a tapestry—a tapestry woven with threads of innovation, empathy, and relentless dedication to excellence. As you embark on this journey, may these narratives inspire, inform, and invigorate your pursuit of customer-centricity, shaping not only existing customer experiences but future experiences yet to unfold.

The intent of this second CX-PRO publication was to take the new customer experience manager beyond the basics that were covered in the first book and nurture them along the path of success within the CX discipline by perspectives and practices shared from learned and experienced CX practitioners and educators.

In embracing the journey of mastering customer experience management, remember that growth comes not only from the accumulation of knowledge but also from the choices we make in how we engage with that knowledge. With each chapter offering a unique perspective and valuable insights, this book empowers you, the reader, to chart your own course towards excellence in the CX discipline.

As you embark on this journey, may the wisdom shared by seasoned practitioners and educators serve as guiding lights, illuminating the path to success. The adventure awaits—begin wherever your curiosity leads you, and may each chapter be a stepping stone towards your ultimate mastery of the art and science of customer experience management.

Chapter 1—Aligning CX with the C-Suite

Patty Soltis, CCXP

"Leaps of greatness require the combined problem-solving ability of people who trust each other"
Simon Senek

Introduction

CX leaders must stop trying to prove ROI and instead add value to the organization and connect to leadership priorities. This is a win for both the organization and CX. In a Gartner survey with CEOs and CFOs, the top priorities are growth, work force management and technology. In this chapter, you will learn about the priorities of the CEO and the CFO and gain a better understanding of their roles and responsibilities. Use this empathy and understanding to drive change for your teams, divisions, and departments, create a CX strategy that aligns with the priorities of leadership, leverage CX and business metrics that translate through the organization, and use storytelling to drive change that leads to results.

Understand the Priorities of the CEO and CFO

The top three priorities according to the Gartner 2023 study for the CEO and CFO are:

1. Growth
2. Workforce
3. Technology

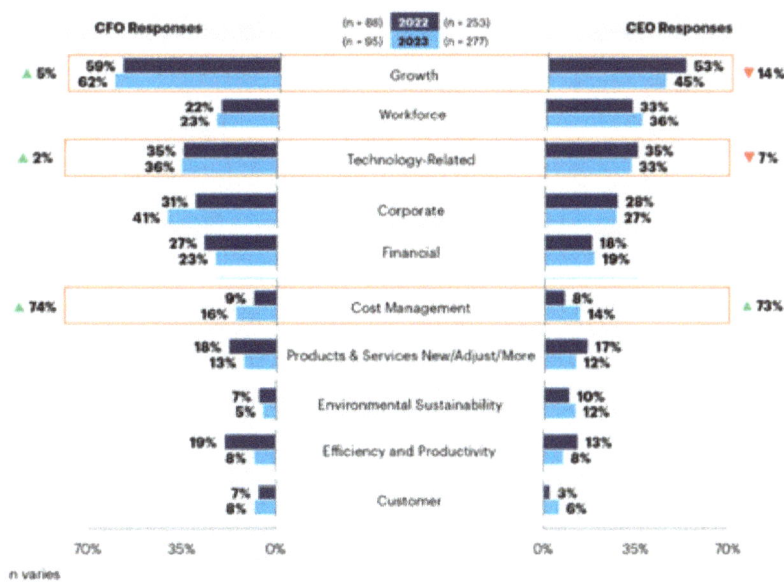

Notice that the customer sits at the bottom of their priority list. However, according to an April 2022 survey data from Harvard Business Review, 88% of executives feel that customer engagement has a significant impact on their organization's bottom line.

Growth Is the Top Priority

CEOs are optimistic about growth in their country, company, and the global economy according to a KPMG 2023 U.S. CEO Outlook.

CEOs Are Investing in Their Workforce

According to the same 2023 KPMG study, 75% of U.S. CEOs agree that a collaborative leadership style enables greater success. And 83% of CEO's say their organization's success, including growth objectives, depends on having a strong ethical culture. However, 36% of CEOs expect a talent decrease according to Summer 2023 Fortune/Deloitte CEO Survey Insights. CEOs are looking for collaborative leadership with shared management and operational responsibilities that communicate values, goals, and progress. CEOs are committed to actively listening to people and acting on their feedback. Talent and culture matter. CEOs are embracing change and innovation while investing in people for upskilling. They reward people who come to the office and build ethical cultures.

Technology is More Than a Buzz Word

Generative AI is expected to improve and accelerate profitability. Business leaders are turning to AI to create greater agility and manage strategic shifts at lighting speeds. According to Summer 2023 Fortune/Deloitte CEO Survey Insights, 79% of CEOs expect Gen AI to increase efficiencies, enhance growth and reduce costs while managing risks.

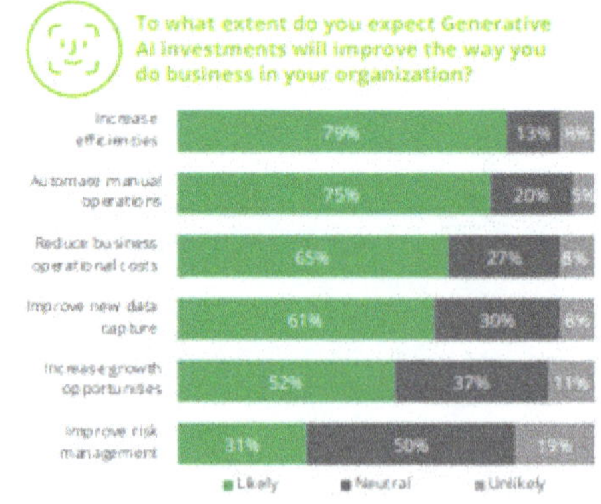

CEOs Experience Many Challenges and Concerns

There are many priorities that CEOs juggle, particularly finding growth in uncertain business climates and balancing strategic understanding. The CEOs role comes down to six elements cited by McKinsey & Company. These six elements spread out to 18 more practices.

Geopolitics sits at the top of their concerns with uncertainty and global inflation—57% indicated geopolitical instability and inflation as a top concern and only 38% are confident in geopolitical instability according to Summer 2023 Fortune/Deloitte CEO Survey Insights. Only 36% of CEOs are confident in the financial/market instability while 53% still expect a recession.

All of this makes growth difficult.

The CFO Role Has Its Own Significant Challenges

The CFO is a strategic partner that contributes to the growth and financial health of the organization. They need to take risks that are well-considered and calculated. They are expected to have a deep knowledge of customers, competitors, and the company's place in the market with a forward-thinking mindset.

CFOs need to provide business cases with the finanical impact and strategic aims within the business cycle. Their communication needs to substantiate the organization's next moves and it must be honest, objective and easily understood avoiding accounting jargon.

CFOs are looking at increasing pricing and cost optimization. Productivity, efficiencies and automation are on their priority list according to the Gartner 2023 study. And the customer is nowhere to be found on their list.

CX Leaders Can Add Value

CX leaders can leverage this information with a greater understanding of what matters to those around them. Use empathy to relate and build CX goals, action, and communication. Build value incorporating the priorities of the C-suite, business unit, department, or division.

This company information is available in many forms and more research needs to be done. Speak with internal partners, read annual reports, analyze roadmaps, listen to CEOs addresses, and more to attain knowledge.

Build on the Organization's Strategy

CX is stymied, the customer is the lowest priority for the CEO and CFO. The customer is not even getting lip service anymore. One in four CX leaders are at risk because they did not connect, Harley Manning repeatedly said this during his time at Forrester.

The smart CX leader will focus on the top priorities—growth, workforce, and technology to add value. Create a CX strategy that is synonymous with these priorities and communicate as a true servant leader to the organization.

Build a CX strategy with a value proposition, focused on the customer needs, using resources and adopting metrics that matter. Add to growth.

Growth and the Impact on the Bottom Line

CX leaders impact growth in four ways:

1. Acquisition
2. Retention
3. CLV (customer lifetime value)
4. Expenses

Build something that draws potential customer in and keeps customer in reducing churn and adding market share. Grow CLV with retention. Increase wallet share with cross selling and building the sale. Improve loyalty and recommendations and more. Reduce expenses with efficiencies, lower marketing costs, improved innovation, increased productivity and retention (both customer and employee).

Building a Value Proposition

Utilize the areas and categories of growth for the organization. Look at the customer segments where this growth will orginate and ignite, determine their priorities from multiple sources of VOC feedback. There are both short term and long term goals and impact from this. Small projects can go a long way. It will take scalability, sustainability, and milestones to make this happen. Determine the needed improvement, time frame, and metrics. Include resources and partners in the organization.

A Value Proposition Example

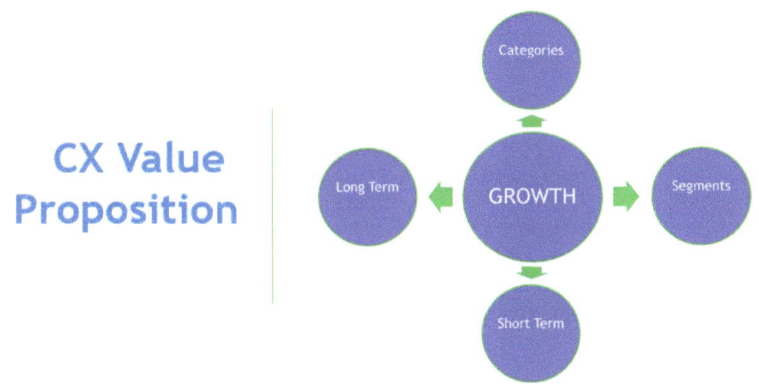

In my retail days, I led stores and set strategic objectives to achieve financial goals, market share and growth. The vision was for the store to be the fashion destination for the community. According to VOC, this mattered to the customer.

To get there, the long term goal was to add exclusive fashion lines to the store. The customers told us what they wanted and the front line was one of the best places to gather this VOC. The short term goal was to add a smaller division of a fashion house with quick successes. The category was to get into the beauty world, grow that successfully and add in shoes, handbags and attire.

There were two customer segments, the aspirational customer and the core customer. Both of these customers could shop in the beauty world enabling success. The aspirational customer could cross into shoes and handbags. The core customer would develop an affinity to purchase in from this designer in shoes, handbags and attire.

A customer strategy was developed using insights and data from VOC and VOE to build the beauty business. The execution of the strategy led to the additional categories in the store. Time frames were set with milestones based on customer activity and excitement. Customer metrics were used that transitioned to financial metrics. That was the value proposition that created the fashion destination and led to growth.

CX Leaders Have Resources

The only way to leverage these resources is to acknowledge them and their usability in the CX strategy and execution.

- Internal resources include: tech, data, insights, partners, human resources.
- External resources include: 3rd party research, trade journals, professional relationships, professional associations, conferences, webinars, podcasts, social media.

These lists are not exhaustive, and doing the research to find resources is necessary. Many CX leaders have a wealth of resources, even if they are not financial and if the CX leader has to influence without authority. Build a system to manage the resources and extrapolate data as needed.

The Many Forms of Customer Data

Consider customer segments and their penetration to the business. Looks a purchase patterns. Go beyond the obvious ways to assess the needs of the customer using all forms of VOC and customer journey maps. There is a wealth of data and information here.

CX leaders need to analyze and action retention, churn and acquisition for both growth and risk. Look at wallet share and market share pulling in the opportunities for both.

Categorize your customers in four categories:
- Maintain—customers that will continue their current spend
- Growth—current customers with the potential to grow wallet share
- Risk—customers with possible decreasing spend
- Opportunity—acquisition customers

Understand the penetration, potential and impact each of these has on the business. Tie them back to product launches, growth and declines. On a larger scale, reviewing revenue and revenue segments presents the opportunity to tie growth to customer segments and their penetration so efforts are laser focused. This is revenue growth.

Leveraging Company Metrics and CX Metrics

Set the scenario for growth and align with the metrics of the organization first. Set it up with the numbers from sales, expenses, net income, COGS (cost of goods sold), operating margin, profit margin, EBITDA. More examples of company metrics are in the graphic below. Each industry has additional company metrics to add in. For example, retailers review sell through, dollars per square foot, average unit sale, items per transaction and more.

Sales	Operating Margin	Selling Cost	Shareholder Returns
Net Income	Profit Margin	Cost of Goods Sold	Share Price
EBITDA	Gross Margin	Working Capital	Shareholder Equity
Expenses	Growth Rate	Cash Flow	Return on Equity

There is an infinite list of CX metrics that can be tied to the company metrics. Use these judiciously to speak the language of the audience and relate the CX value. Adapting metrics from partners and relating them to CX metrics is always helpful.

Connecting Company Metrics to CX Metrics

In retail, the goal is meet or exceed profit goals. The only way to do that was to exceed gross margin goals (Sales-COGS=Gross Margin). That meant that sell throughs needed to be achieved. Sell through is how quickly merchandise is sold from its arrival in the store—and at regular price without any markdowns or promotional pricing. Two factors weighed on sell through. One was productivity of the selling team. This was based on a number of factors and all related to the employee experience as shown in the figure below. The other factor was conversion, converting the shoppers who entered into the store into purchasing.

Traffic came in the store to experience an enjoyable shoppping experience. CX metrics drove traffic with market share from customer retention and referrals. Based on the satisfaction from NPS and CSAT, traffic would increase or decrease. At the conversion point, there was something crucial that happened. Store CSAT metrics focused the store team on ensuring a quick greeting and creating a welcoming atmosphere for shoppers. If a shopper felt welcome in the store, the possibility of purchasing increased. That fueled productivity.

Both conversion and productivity led to greater sell throughs and gross margin. Higher customer satisfaction drove cross sell opportunities and increased wallet share with higher average unit sale (AUS) and items per transaction (IPT). Economic rate of return (ERR) increased and NPS metrics were tied to sales dollars and percentages. That led to increased profits. CX metrics connected directly to the organization's metrics.

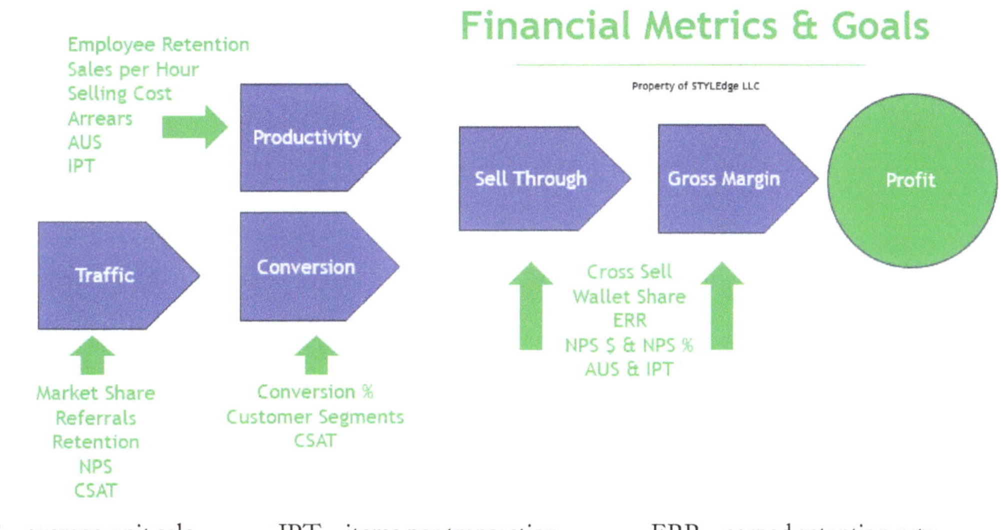

AUS—average unit sale   IPT—items per transaction   ERR—earned retention rate

Compel Action With Storytelling

Without an effective call to action, the CX strategy will go nowhere. Think about what action you are trying to evoke, what feeling you are tapping into and what problems you solve. Know your business, know your numbers and make it relational. Tie in the data without reading numbers, focus on the most important aspects to make it actionable, and limit how much data you share to make it more memorable and quotable.

Adding the customer voice into this is necessary. That could be an audio or video clip or a series of meaningful quotes. Let your audience feel the emotion and, if possible, make it personal to the audience. If you can make it visual, do so. Show the percentages. For example, if it is a 20% customer loss, have them look around the room and take 20% of the people out.

If you can't be in the room, leverage your colleagues and partners. Prepare them with a story that will compel action, understand the risk, and create growth. It's advisable to have mini stories on hand to convincingly share whenever the opportunity arises. These elevator pitches can grab someone's attention.

Creating Alignment

Invest time in building the value proposition with growth categories and customer segments, then add in the short and long term goals. Always keep in mind scability, sustainabilily, milestones and time frames. Build and use your list of resources both internally and externally. Look at the gaps to identify additonal resources including partnerships. Constantly assess and reassess the customers needs. Look at the tools and data used to assess the customer needs, and how this information can be aligned to the company goals and growth. Make a list of the company metrics and tie your CX metrics to them—not the other way around. This list could change for both organizational and CX metrics, it should be revisited. Wrap it all up and communicate to compel action. Build the story with what matters to your partners, teams, leaders and organization. Tie this back to growth creation and the north star of the organization. Adapt as needed to be agile and able to pivot.

Chapter 2—CX From a Frontline Perspective

Scott Gilbey

> *"Employee loyalty begins with employer loyalty. Your employees should know that if they do the job they were hired to do with a reasonable amount of competence and efficiency, you will support them."*
>
> **Harvey Mackay**

(Author's caveat: "Should" is the operative word. What are you doing to help your employees be competent?)

In this chapter, you'll learn about some personal experience observations and recommendations from the frontline; observations made by an hourly worker, low on the corporate hierarchy. Over a 30-month period from late 2021 through early 2024, this worker was hired and onboarded on five separate occasions by five different employers including three retailers, an airline, and a public-school board. Additionally, an 18-month journey as a surgery and rehab patient adds a corroborating perspective from the frontline of healthcare.

Prior to 2021, this frontline worker had a professional background in business, most recently as Senior Vice President, Customer Experience & Service Offering, with a global portfolio that encompassed sales processes, product management, marketing, communications, change management, master data governance, business model transformation, digitalization, plus an assortment of executive level special projects ranging from the granularity of post-acquisition mergers to the broad strategic scope of training and development programs.

Armed with the above business background, plus a recent CCXP certification, and deep curiosity of the human condition, let's go to the frontline and see what's happening there.

The Experience Gap

The experience gap (delivery gap, Bain & Company, 2005) is well known amongst the Customer Experience (CX) community: 80% of CEOs say they deliver great experience, whereas only 8% of customers agree, as illustrated in the chart.

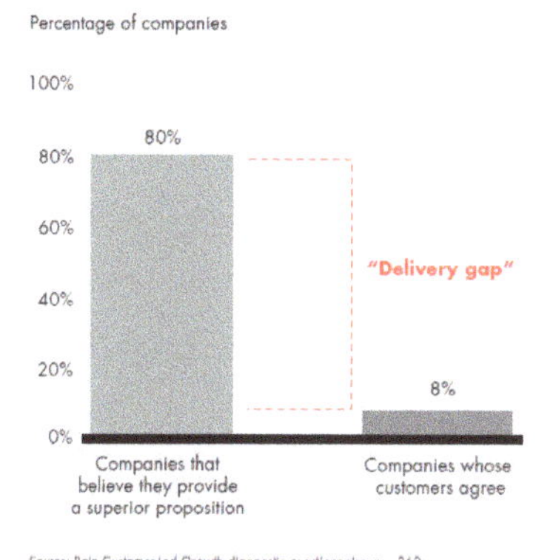

The original delivery gap findings can be summarized as the difference between the desired customer experience and the actual delivered experience. More specifically:

- Bain found that CEOs often overestimated the quality of service their companies were delivering. They believed they were providing excellent service based on internal metrics and feedback.
- On the other hand, customers were often dissatisfied with the actual service they received. Despite companies' efforts to meet customer needs, there was a noticeable gap between customer expectations and the actual delivered experience.

Bain emphasized the importance of closing this gap to improve customer satisfaction, loyalty, and ultimately business performance. A broader understanding of the Experience Gap includes the disparity between the skill of individuals and departments and the skill required in the workforce or in specific roles and functions.

The Gap is fueled by employee attrition, rapid technological advancements, changing industry demands, and shortcomings in training and development. None of this is new or surprising. Similar findings have been published over the years. The numbers may change, but the skew never does. Overwhelmingly, and consistently, company leaders tend to think more of themselves than do customers.

Separately, in 2021, Watermark Consulting published a different benchmark study focusing on the return on investment (ROI) of Customer Experience. They looked at thirteen years of data (2007 through 2019), analyzing cumulative stock returns against publicly available third-party customer experience rankings.

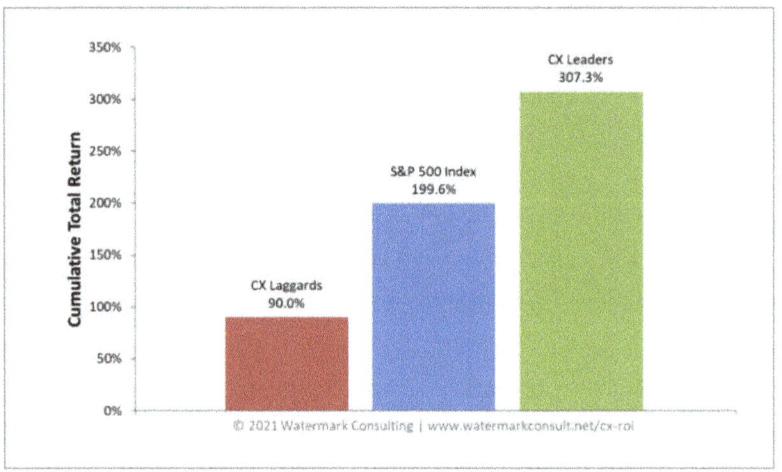

SOURCE: Watermark Consulting

Watermark concluded that "many business leaders pay lip service to the concept of customer experience—publicly affirming its importance, but privately skeptical of its value." And more, "The study vividly illustrates the vital role customer experience plays in business success."

The report nicely summarizes the key attributes of CX Leading Companies:
- They aim for more than customer satisfaction.
- They leave nothing to chance.
- They shape memories, not just experiences.
- They infuse the experience with emotional resonance.
- They focus on both the customer and the employee experience.

Now, in 2024, we have a continuous stream of AI-generated thought-leadership extolling the virtues of experience even as large companies cycle through layoffs of CX leaders and culling of entire Experience Departments.

Side note—It's been reported that the average tenure for customer experience leaders is between 12 to 24 months (cmswire.com), not far from the average tenure for Chief Marketing Officers, holding steady at 40 months, according to Spencer Stuart. Separately, McKinsey & Company asserts that "re-wiring" a company to an experience mindset is typically a two- to four-year journey. In each of these circumstances, the project lasts longer than the people.

The Experience Gap is a real thing that cannot be denied. I wondered what ChatGPT might have to say about it.

Prompt: What is the experience gap, as discussed within the Customer Experience community?

Reply:

- In the context of the Customer Experience (CX) community, the experience gap refers to the difference between the customer's expectations and the actual experience they have with a product, service, or brand. This concept is central to understanding and improving customer satisfaction and loyalty.
- The experience gap arises when there is a mismatch between what customers anticipate or desire from their interactions with a company and what they receive. This can occur at various touchpoints along the customer journey, including pre-purchase, purchase, and post-purchase stages.
- For instance, if a customer expects prompt and helpful customer service but encounters long wait times and unresponsive support representatives, there is a noticeable experience gap. Similarly, if a product's features or performance falls short of what was promised in marketing materials, it can lead to dissatisfaction and widen the experience gap.

In the CX community, addressing the Experience Gap involves identifying areas where customer expectations are not being met and implementing strategies to bridge that divide. This may include improving communication channels, enhancing product quality, providing better training for customer-facing staff, and gathering feedback to continually refine and optimize the customer experience. By closing the experience gap, companies can foster stronger relationships with customers and drive long-term success.

Why is this Gap so pervasive, and so persistent? Legions of consultants say it's about strategy, mission, vision, values, culture, hiring practices, technology, empathy, roadmaps, etc. That was my view too from the Boardroom of a multi-billion-dollar, global industrial company operating in 50 countries. Now I find myself cycling through a variety of hourly paid frontline gigs, and my perspective of the business world, and its take on experience, has evolved. Something is missing. While I do not have "the" answer, I do have "an" answer. It's at the frontline.

What is "Frontline?"

Rather than recreate what is generally known, we can simply use our keyboard for a search of "frontline."

Dictionary.com—Relating to, or suitable for the front line of a military formation: frontline troops. Public service and business employees who are in direct contact with the public: frontline staff, to the fore; advanced, conspicuous.

> *Merriam-Webster.com*—1a: a military line formed by the most advanced tactical combat units. 1b: an area of potential or actual conflict or struggle. 2: the most advanced, responsible, or visible position in a field or activity.
>
> *Dictionary.cambridge.org*—An employee who deals directly with customers, or who is directly involved in making a product. A manager whose job involves dealing directly with a group of employees.

The term "Frontline" has a military origin. There are direct parallels with business, especially as they relate to advanced contact, being conspicuously visible and responsible, as well as elements of potential or actual struggle. While this is the reality at the Frontline, many organizations tend to take their Frontline for granted, oversimplifying the impact of their work. Some companies seem to forget that customer-facing employees play a pivotal role in shaping customer experiences.

<u>My definition of Frontline</u>: any aspect of a company, be it person, machine, or technology, which interacts with customers, human employees being the most substantial. These interactions are primarily on-stage and can be off-stage too; out of sight must not be out of mind.

I am a frontline person myself, and the essence of this chapter is all about people. At the same time, please consider that the retail self-checkout register, security swipes and scanners, and the airport kiosk are also frontline; the person or chatbot at a call center too! I work alongside this technology and these devices. They have a huge impact on my day and therefore a huge impact on the customer experience.

COMPETENCE

As a frontline worker, I want to be competent, and I want to be seen to be competent. According to a Washington Post Ipsos poll from March 2023, most (61%) workers say they try to excel in their jobs; 33% say they do their job well but don't go beyond what they're paid to do. Only 4% say they're doing just enough to get by. Much of this is in response to how the employer treats their employees.

Don't assume I am unmotivated. Don't shower me with fake empathy. Instead, help me to be competent. I want to know the 10 to 20 specific tasks I need to perform each day. I want to be good at those tasks. Otherwise, my interactions with customers can be ad hoc and awkward; frustrating for the customer and embarrassing for me. Watching videos will not make me competent. More on this later.

Surprisingly, however, I am not required to be competent! **This is my #1 observation from 30 months at the frontline.** It does not mean I am NOT competent. It means that supervision is entirely focused on my being compliant and obedient. Whether I am competent at my job does not seem to matter.

"No way," you say! "Yes way," I answer. In each of my five frontline engagements, without exception, what I *do* during the day with customers is rarely acknowledged or questioned. What matters is when I *clock-in*, when I *clock-out*, and where I stand or otherwise *position* myself during my shift.

It begins on Day One, with onboarding. During my recent frontline work, I have been onboarded five times by five great companies across three vastly different businesses: retail, airlines, and public education. Each company has a strong brand, fantastic people, superb products, excellent service, and top financial or operational results.

In each of my five Frontline gigs, my onboarding has been big on marketing and socialization. Each brand instills pride in the new employee. I meet nice people. I hear stories. It feels good. There are policies I must learn and vocabulary to be ingrained. On the other hand, the structural onboarding in terms of learning the job I am required to perform leaves vast opportunities for improvement.

Following are my frontline task-related observations about onboarding:

LMS video training: I log hour upon hour for online training and hundreds of video snippets. Production quality is high. The brand message is strong. Learning is low because I don't yet understand the context and basic vocabulary. "Just do it," said one supervisor. LMS videos are efficient for sharing mass information. Without identifying and practicing essential tasks, video learning is low and fades quickly.

Frontline peers: It has been my hourly on-the-clock peers from whom I've learned the day-to-day details of my job, the keystrokes, how to avoid trouble, and how to be successful. When in need, eight times out of ten I ask a peer before a supervisor because, on average, my peer group is more helpful and more empathetic than a typical supervisor.

Onboarding checklists: Every company has checklists. They are essential. But I have not seen them used as designed or intended. I asked one supervisor to review my checklist and the response was essentially, "don't waste my time". At another, I attempted to book a 90-day review with a manager but could not because the activity had already (unbeknownst to me) been marked as completed.

Ad Hoc Tribal Knowledge: This is how I learn to do the critical tasks of my Frontline job. Period! Whether ordering a piece of 2x4 lumber, searching for lost luggage, or providing substitute lessons in school, there is zero practice before I interact with customers, zero. I simply jump in and figure it out, leaning on peers as needed and if available. Over time, the tasks gradually become familiar. Familiarity is one thing. Competence is quite another.

The honeymoon period: During my first 10 or so days, I am considered fragile and new. Next is a period of 30 to 90 days when I am simply new. One day I am suddenly expected to know and do everything, whether my capability has been validated or not. As a mature person I can manage the honeymoon. Unfortunately, I have seen others, both young and experienced, struggle and talk of quitting even while their onboarding is underway.

A fellow Frontliner, Jim and I started at a retailer about the same time. Our two weeks of LMS training overlapped by a few days. We met while hunched side-by-side over a shared laptop tucked into a corner of the store manager's office. A few months later I decided to cut the words "In Training" from my name badge. I showed Jim. He laughed and said, "I'm staying 'in training' forever. That way I don't have to explain to customers why I don't know what I'm doing." True story.

Many companies will say their onboarding is strategic and well thought out. Please think again! Most companies are rightly concerned about CX and EX. At the same time, widely published data show an alarming trend of low employee engagement and an increasing experience gap between boardroom strategy and frontline reality.

The Gap begins on day one with onboarding. I'm here and I see it. It can be different. It must be better.

If you want to increase employee engagement and decrease attrition, start at the beginning. Look hard at your onboarding. Help your employees become competent. That's what we want and expect.

SUPERVISION

At the frontline, on the floor, big box retail, hardware store, airport baggage service, anywhere, I run into unique customer challenges every day, all day long. I say, "I'm sorry, I don't know the answer to this problem. But I will find out quickly."

To whom do you think I turn?
If I need PERMISSION … supervisor.
If I need RULES … headquarters.
If I need HELP … peer.

I rarely look up. Instead, I look sideways. If I need help, to learn something, or solve a problem, I ask a frontline peer, without exception, every time. My frontline peers are the strength in my day.

Part of the challenge has to do with supervisory skills. My supervisors tend to be good people. Good companies attract good people. However, being a good person does not automatically make one a good supervisor. The personal behavior of a supervisor reflects the company brand and can support or degrade onboarding. Their actions, words, availability, empathy, and job knowledge deeply impact my attitude and effectiveness as a new employee.

An even larger part of the challenge has to do with the purpose of Supervision in the first place. Supervisors are frontliners too. They learn their tasks and assume behaviors on the fly as I do. It is the brand, the company, that determines the role of the Supervision layer in their organization.

This is my #2 observation from 30 months at the frontline. More of a question. What is the purpose of Frontline Supervision in the organizational layer? Imagine, instead of expending time and energy on compliance and obedience, your Front Supervision was single-mindedly focused on helping the Frontline be competent, to help each other serve customers. "Servant Leadership" comes to mind. The experience gap would shrink!

DATA

One afternoon at the Special Services Desk …

"I don't want $50; I want my window."

40 minutes earlier …
The customer was a home builder. A regular patron of a building supplies retailer. It was the customer's third attempt to pick up and complete an order of seven windows for a construction job.

FRONTLINER: I am sorry, we can't find your order.
CUSTOMER: Find it or call a manager to explain.

(Frontliner calls the manager for backup)
MANAGER: What's the problem?
FRONTLINER: We cannot find the customer's window.
MANAGER: Give the customer a $50 discount.
FRONTLINER: We can give you a $50 discount.
CUSTOMER: I don't want $50; I want my window.

The above is a condensed version of a real event. The company has a good strategy, strong technology, and great people. This sort of thing happens on a recurring basis, feeding the ever-present experience gap. As CX professionals, let's confidently get into the data weeds, into the details. That is where so much opportunity lies hidden, waiting to be revealed.

Experience Is a Bell Curve

Much of CX occurs in the extremes of good or bad, in the long tails of a normal distribution. Outlier examples of uniquely superb CX and EX are easy to find. The unintended consequence can be complacency, "We are so good." Same for uniquely bad examples, "They are so bad".

The Bain delivery gap and the Watermark leader-laggard study themselves drew large conclusions from small sample sizes.

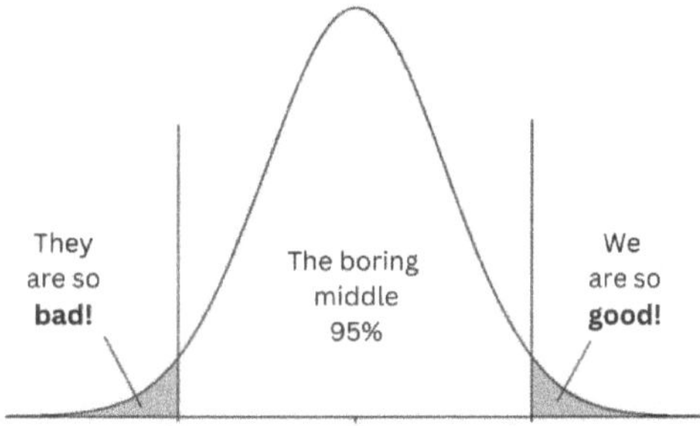

This is my #3 observation from 30 months at the frontline. Most daily interactions live in the boring middle of the bell curve where they don't garner much attention. Outliers get the spotlight. Therein lies a secret to breaking the mystery of the CX/EX gap—spend the bulk of your effort fixing average, the boring middle.

Conclusions

Look up in the sky.
Is it a Gap?
Is it a Chasm?
No … it's an EXPERIENCE HALLUCINATION

Many CX people are familiar with the experience gap (80%/8%) originally penned by Bain. And still, the word "gap" doesn't sufficiently explain the distance between what the boardroom thinks is happening at the frontline and what is happening. It is sometimes called a "chasm." The Experience Gap is on full display here at the frontline. But it's hard to see.

Part of the problem is that Customer Experience has the following characteristics:
- It's easy to talk about. Everyone has a valid opinion, with stark examples of good and bad.
- Its terms of reference are fragmented and not universally defined.
- It's often difficult to quantify except in a scholarly way or with aggregate numbers.

Summary—The Experience Gap has Three Dimensions at the Frontline

The "Frontline Experience Gap" persists across industries, undermining brand reputation and customer loyalty. While this gap has been acknowledged for years, its resolution remains elusive. However, a closer examination reveals that a solution lies at the frontline, where competence, supervision, and data converge to shape customer interactions. Consider each of the following potential solutions to bridge each respective gap.

The Competence Gap

Frontline employees often embark on their roles armed with theoretical knowledge from learning management systems (LMS) but lack practical experience. This results in situations where employees struggle to perform basic tasks, leading to customer dissatisfaction and employee frustration. The prevailing approach to training, focused on participation rather than skill acquisition, exacerbates this issue. To bridge the competence gap, companies must prioritize hands-on training and real-world practice, ensuring that frontline staff are equipped with the necessary skills to excel in their roles.

The Supervision Gap

While frontline employees seek guidance and support from their supervisors, they often encounter a lack of effective leadership. Supervisors, burdened with compliance responsibilities and performance metrics, prioritize tasks over mentorship. As a result, frontline workers turn to their peers for assistance, bypassing the supervision layer. To address this gap, companies must redefine the role of supervision, emphasizing mentorship and skill development rather than blindly focusing on compliance and obedience. By empowering supervisors to function as "Servant Leaders," companies can foster a culture of continuous learning and improvement at the frontline.

The Data Gap

In today's data-driven landscape, frontline employees are inundated with information, much of which is irrelevant to their immediate tasks. This "data deluge" distracts employees from their core responsibilities and hampers decision-making. Moreover, frontline staff often lack access to critical data (e.g., inventory) that could enhance customer interactions. To overcome the data gap, companies must provide frontline employees with specific and relevant data tailored to their roles and the task at hand. Deal with outliers but don't be overly distracted by them.

Integration and Action

Finally, to bridge the Frontline Experience Gap, companies must adopt an integrated approach that addresses the three dimensions of competence, supervision, and data integration. This requires a shift in mindset, prioritizing employee skills and empowerment. By investing in hands-on training, fostering supportive supervision, and streamlining data delivery, companies can transform their frontline operations to deliver consistently exceptional customer experiences in an increasingly competitive landscape.

> *"Employees who believe that management is concerned about them as a whole person—not just an employee—are more productive, more satisfied, more fulfilled. Satisfied employees mean satisfied customers, which leads to profitability."*
>
> Anne M. Mulcahy

Chapter 3—Building CX Resiliency Through Self-Care

Jerry Seufert

> *"Individual commitment to a group effort–that is what makes a team work, a company work, a society work, a civilization work."*
>
> **Vince Lombardi**

Nurturing the CX Professional—Cultivating Self-Care and Growth in a Challenging Landscape

Do not skip this chapter. Well, you might say, that's an odd way to begin a chapter in a professional book. Yet in key respects, on a personal level this may be the most important chapter in the book. Why? As a small group moderator, coach, advisor, and organizer of multiple CX community groups I've been privileged to be part of thousands of conversations with CX professionals around the globe from all walks of the community at differing stages of their working lives. ***To get right to the point, many CX professionals don't practice healthy self-care or proactively manage their professional and personal growth in accordance with their needs and talents and the world within which they apply their craft.***

Additionally, many CX professionals operate in small teams or as individual contributors apart from the core of their organizations. Buffeted by economic headwinds and job loss, to be frank, it is not a great time to be a CX professional, yet the need is still there and the call to serve is strong. In this chapter we will explore how CX professionals can think about their professional lives and the 'inner space' that provides the sturdy platform upon which to build and to become valued contributors and community members now and in the future.

In my work I have noticed six key ways CX folks need to take better care of themselves and their careers:

1. Enlisting one's mind as an ally.
2. Being a good steward of one's body.
3. Curating one's own journey.
4. Asking for and offering help.
5. Being a scientist and systems-thinker in one's work.
6. Stepping away from a soloist mentality and embracing community.

In each section below, I have included some helpful resources. Links are valid as of May 2024; many have newsletters you can sign up for.

Before beginning, I invite you to consider using each topic as encouragement to visualize the 'future you,' your contributions to the community as 'future you,' and the cumulative influence of a community that has also taken this journey. This is called *'protopian'* thinking. Protopia refers to a society that, rather than solving all its problems (as in a utopia) or falling into dire dysfunction (as in a dystopia), makes incremental progress over a long period of time. My hope here is not to provide answers, but to help everyone to build a stronger foundation upon which to ask great questions and then work out solutions together. Imagine a more creative, influential, effective, stronger, and resilient community. For inspiration on this theme, look at a series currently airing on public TV, *A Brief History of the Future*.

https://www.pbs.org/show/a-brief-history-of-the-future/

Additionally, I encourage everyone to use community resources to talk about these things together in positive and protopian ways. Through discussions on the CXPA Forum, local network meetups, and whenever you gather, focus on the bright future you can create together.

A Sturdy, Resilient Self Begins in the Mind

One's mind is the captain of their ship. Yet the combined effect of world events, a global pandemic, and industry upheaval have left many CX professionals unstable, anxious, and unsure what tomorrow may bring. Needless to say, no one is at their best under these conditions. So, the very first thing is to retake the mind. Eliminate distractions from social media; remember, it's designed to distract you so someone else can profit. Every time you are tempted to post online content, ask yourself why and for whose benefit. If not clear then the default reason is to induce traffic so the platform can generate revenue, and only you can decide if you want to play along.

Learn at least basic meditation and mindfulness so you can stay in control and be at your best. Don't sabotage your mind by poor self-care (see below). An exhausted body does not think well. With fewer distractions and better care your mind opens itself up to fresh nourishment. Listen, notice, ask questions. Read widely and intentionally especially from works outside the core CX community and topics and books that stretch you and not just confirm what you already know. Indulge your curiosity, visit your library, wander through a bookstore, ask folks what they are reading.

Too often folks focus primarily on what others are doing and seek to learn from 'masters.' Socrates taught that wisdom doesn't arise from downloading a body of knowledge from teacher to student, but in a compassionate voice helping one to learn to think for oneself. But in its natural state one's mind tends to wander and lose focus; therefore, we need to learn and hone skills in self-management.

Look at 'Top 50' lists—whether they be books, podcasts, influencers, or events—with a critical eye towards how using your precious time will be served. In the future you will be rewarded and gratified based on your impact in the world, not what podcasts you listened to.

Have a personal philosophy. That's a loaded phrase and too often people reject it, proclaiming: "That's for college professors," "What could the words of long dead thinkers possible mean to me?" or "Who has time to think, I've got things to do!" Yet its relevance is clear by revisiting the four definitions according to Meriam Webster:

1. The study of the basic ideas about knowledge, truth, right and wrong, religion, and the nature and meaning of life.
2. The philosophical teachings or principles of a person or group.
3. The general principles of a field of study or activity.
4. Someone's basic beliefs about the way people should live.

In my experience most people focus in on definition 2; think of the Greek philosophers, Kant, Nietzsche, etc. But a closer look at definitions 1, 3, and 4 reveals that philosophy is an intentional activity of the mind, much as exercise is an activity of the body. Therefore, one can grow in wisdom by engaging in thinking about life and work. And like we must exercise for the sake of the body; we must think to deepen our understanding and grow in wisdom *by thinking*. Similarly, as when we don't exercise our bodies decline in fitness and health, our minds are built to think and when we neglect that process our philosophy suffers and our wisdom stagnates or becomes subject to disruptions.

Below are a few resources I refer to weekly.

The School of Life	https://www.theschooloflife.com/	Practical insights for living today
Philosophy Break	https://philosophybreak.com/	Short essays delivered to your in-box
Greater Good Magazine	https://greatergood.berkeley.edu/	Science-backed insights into happiness and meaningful living

Take Care of Your Body and Health

We are—even our minds—organic and require constant maintenance and nurturing. Failure to faithfully take care of one's body will inevitably lead to declined performance, failures, and even death. Self-care includes body, mind, and spirit. Neglect any of these and it will hurt, possibly a lot. There are many great resources available for each, but very simply it can be thought of intersecting aspects of a fully well person. For example, a strong and healthy body that is nourished, gets rest, and is active sustains a positive, prosocial outlook. Such a healthy outlook in turn facilitates a strong and resilient spirit. And thereby refreshed and nourished, one can think clearly and creatively.

Be More Resilient to Disruptions, Industry Mood Swings, and Job Loss.

A CX professional without work is truly a loss for everyone, beginning with self and family but also community. Without work, the CX professional is not helping any organization, not fully participating in the community, not growing, not buying CX services and education, and gradually becoming less relevant. As a connected ecosystem, *the entire community suffers when even one person loses their work*. Have a personal road map and always know what you would do if you suddenly lost your job. Build support systems before you need them—friends, groups, etc.

Tragically, most only start looking when they have lost work. Instead, pivot to a mindset that you are *always* looking for. What does 'looking' mean today? Networking, lots of networking. Being part of a job seekers small group for networking, tips and techniques, companionship, and to protect your mental health. Quit insisting that your next job has the words 'customer experience' in it and focus instead on the work you want to do and where it's being done regardless of the title, something you only learn through personal networking. Flip your emphasis from looking at job boards, (much of which is imaginative at best) and on-line applications and recommit to personal networking as your primary strategy. And if you do lose your work and then find something new, remember to pay it forward to those still on the hamster wheel that is, as folks euphemistically say, 'in transition.'

The CX Community is Extraordinarily Generous

Too many CX professionals don't ask and spend a lot of time reinventing the wheel. Be an experiences, tools, and frameworks collector and share what you learn. The surest way to get help is to be of help; give and get. In 2024 there is great content on-line, so much so that is no longer a search for *anything*, but a process of discernment figuring out what is original and rock solid vs. which is repetitive or derivative. For this you need folks you trust and you also need to be a trusted source. The authors of this book exemplify this thinking, having contributed rock solid content not for notoriety, but to lift the community. Also set aside the mostly inconsequential bickering and 'one upmanship' on social media and cooperate.

Be a Scientist and a Systems Thinker

Too often I see CX professionals struggle with understanding when to use what tools, how and why they work, and when to look for or build new ones. This can be very frustrating and lead to errors. A simple example: Not understanding statistical validity can lead to unsupported conclusions from survey research.

A root cause for this in my view is a lack of appreciation for scientific methods and systems thinking. Together they are the foundation for almost everything CX pro's do when they are at their best.

The scientific method is an empirical method for acquiring knowledge that has characterized the development of science since at least the 17th century. The scientific method involves careful observation coupled with rigorous skepticism, because cognitive assumptions can distort the interpretation of the observation. Scientific inquiry includes creating a hypothesis through inductive reasoning, testing it through experiments and statistical analysis, and adjusting or discarding the hypothesis based on the results.

Systems thinking is a way of making sense of the complexity of the world by looking at it in terms of wholes and relationships rather than by splitting it down into its parts. It has been used as a way of exploring and developing effective action in complex contexts, enabling systems change. Systems thinking draws on and contributes to systems theory and the system sciences.

Together they tie together observation, experimentation, documenting knowledge, and applying knowledge to real problems, and are the foundation of other tools like engineering and change management. So be curious and always learn. Spend *much* more time where the work is done talking to the people that do that work and the customers you find there. Get familiar with a set of engineering and user research techniques such as 'going to Gemba,' ethnography, and perspective getting (much more powerful than empathy, interestingly). Consider getting a degree in a STEM discipline known for its rigor. The Michigan State University Master's Degree in Customer Experience Management (MSU-CXM) is setting the pace but is not the only option.

Everyone gets busy and, without realizing it, many get out on an island without a canoe.

This is the classic 'boil the frog' syndrome and many wake up one day and ask, "how did I get here?" Healthy CX professionals need to have community in many ways. Professional groups. Small groups. Fun groups. Personal networking. Workplace coalitions. Hanging out in the break room at the office. Workplace affinity groups (if none, start one). Kitchen cabinets of 'friendlies.' Community groups. Service groups. And friends; when asked most people say they have few, many men say none.

Get Connected

Being connected is not optional or a 'nice to have,' it is essential to mental health, and mental health makes us human and able to do great things. Being connected and in community is the ultimate secret weapon of humans. And lack of connection with the business and finance leaders at your workplace is the root cause of much of why CX is viewed as not valuable and core and no amount of Power Points will fix this. I have been asked what is the right 'amount' of community to which I say there is never too much and only you can say. I meet in at least three groups weekly, at times more, and have several in-person one-on-ones each week. And for my introvert friends, you are not excluded—find community among fellow introverts; there is community for everyone when you look.

Closing Thoughts

This too shall pass and the future is human. By being stronger and more resilient CX professionals can reduce anxiety and open their minds to the kind of creative and novel thinking the community needs to show its true potential and value.

Consider thoughtfully doing these six things:

1. Reclaim your mind.
2. Mind your health and wellness.
3. Harden your working life against disruption.
4. Ask for and give help.
5. Be a scientist and systems thinker.
6. Seek community and connection.

The CX community has much to offer, yet we live and work in tough times for the community. Standing together as strong humans there is nothing beyond the community. There is much work to do and it is upon each member of the community to take care of themselves so all can be stronger together. An old saying has it that 'we are only as strong as our weakest link,' and upon each of us is the opportunity to lift the person next to us and have them lift us up also.

Also remember that the future is in our hands, individually and collectively. Will it be a better CX world than this one, or are we in a doom spiral as several commenters have suggested? Only we can decide, the power is yours—use it wisely. And because one should always live their values, please reach out to me at any time to talk about any of this.

Chapter 4—Delivering on the Customer Service Experience (CSX)

Alex Mead

> *"Customer service is not a department. It's a philosophy to be embraced by everyone in every department!"*
>
> **Shep Hyken**

Leaders define the culture of an organization. The way employees are treated will be felt on the outside by customers.

Introduction

Within the intricate tapestry of customer experience (CX) and CX management, the realm of customer service experience stands as a linchpin—a vital touchpoint where the promises of marketing meet the realities of customer interactions. In this chapter, we embark on a journey through the nuances of delivering exceptional customer service experiences, recognizing its pivotal role in fostering loyalty, driving satisfaction, and safeguarding the long-term viability of businesses. Anchored by a framework that prioritizes a People-First Attitude, Technical and Critical Problem-Solving Skills, and Personal and Professional Skills, we explore the multifaceted dimensions of customer service excellence, illuminated by real-world examples and actionable insights. As the cartoon and quotation above from Shep Hyken suggests, the customer service experience is a shared responsibility among all people within all departments that serve the customer whether directly or indirectly. Often, it's the CSX that determines the overall CX.

Understanding the Customer Service Experience (CSX)

Understanding the Customer Service Experience (CSX) is essential for differentiating it from the broader concept of Customer Experience (CX). CSX focuses on the specific interactions and services provided to customers, which can significantly influence their overall perception of a brand.

For years now, there have been mixed messages about the difference between Customer Service and Customer Experience. Customer Service is often viewed as what happens after a purchase or when something goes wrong, whereas Customer Experience encompasses all interactions with a brand across every lifecycle stage and touchpoint.

Leading CX experts advise that focusing on delivering performance improvements across the entire CX spectrum is more important than worrying about customer service alone. However, to improve CX, one must first measure every aspect of it, leading to the growth of CX survey culture driven by metrics like NPS, CSAT, and Customer Effort. Additionally, journey mapping is often proposed as fundamental to driving CX innovation. Despite these initiatives, both Customer Service and Customer Experience have deteriorated over the past decade, as evidenced by various research papers and personal experiences from industry leaders.

A critical examination reveals that an integrated comprehensive approach to fixing CX by addressing it is flawed. CX is an outcome of various factors and should be approached by separating its components: Brand & Marketing Experience (BMX) and Customer Service Experience (CSX). Combining these elements over 20 years ago created confusion and hindered progress.

Evaluating CX and CSX Principles

It can be argued that addressing Customer Experience holistically may not always be effective. Instead, breaking down the problem into component parts might reveal the biggest issues. Notably, Customer Experience is an outcome influenced by various factors and should be divided into distinct areas that require separate approaches. This distinction, originally blurred by experts, is crucial for effective CX management.

Two Key Areas of Customer Experience

1. **Brand & Marketing Experience (BMX)**:
   - Customer experiences start with brand advertisements across various media.
   - Marketing messages, including emails, social media interactions, and website pop-ups, shape initial perceptions.
   - The physical product experience, packaging, and initial use, such as opening a product or experiencing a service (like a flight or hotel stay), further influence this experience.
2. **Customer Service Experience (CSX)**:
   - CSX includes how easily a customer can place, inquire about, change, receive, or return an order.
   - Effective CSX involves proactive and reactive service, providing effortless, respectful, and engaging interactions throughout the service cycle.

Distinction and Leadership in CSX

Separating BMX and CSX in CX strategies is essential. Often, Marketing Leaders are rebranded as Chief Customer Officers or Chief Experience Officers, which can lead to deteriorating customer service. CSX requires focused leadership by those who understand the high expectations of modern customers, emphasizing personalization and low effort.

CSX can be defined as providing customers with seamless, respectful, and engaging experiences during any interaction with a brand. A service cycle is any stage where a customer interacts with a brand, covering pre-sale, purchase, and post-purchase stages. These interactions should be seamless across all channels, providing proactive and dynamic information updates.

The BMX involves all interactions with the brand's marketing efforts, from ads to packaging. Conversely, CSX focuses on the ease of customer interactions during the service cycle, including order placement, inquiries, and issue resolution. The mistake many CX strategies make is mixing BMX and CSX, often resulting in marketing leaders taking over CX roles and neglecting customer service improvements.

CSX requires clear leadership from those who understand the high service expectations in today's personalized and low-effort customer interactions. CSX is about providing effortless, respectful, and engaging experiences throughout the service cycle, requiring proactive and reactive customer service options. This leads us to the framework around achieving customer service excellence.

People-First Attitude: Putting Customers at the Center

In the realm of customer service excellence, the concept of a People-First Attitude transcends mere rhetoric—it's a guiding principle that shapes every interaction, decision, and strategy. At its core, a People-First Attitude is a profound commitment to prioritizing customers' needs, preferences, and emotions more than anything else. It embodies empathy, compassion, and a relentless dedication to fostering meaningful connections with customers.

Understanding Customer Needs

Central to a People-First Attitude is the ability to empathize with customers—to see the world through their eyes, understand their pain points, and anticipate their desires. This requires active listening, curiosity, and a genuine desire to empathize with customers' experiences. By soliciting feedback, conducting user research, and analyzing customer data, businesses can gain invaluable insights into the diverse needs and preferences of their customer base.

Responsive Communication

Effective communication lies at the heart of a People-First Attitude. Timely, transparent, and empathetic communication fosters trust, reduces anxiety, and enhances overall customer satisfaction. Whether it's responding to inquiries, addressing concerns, or providing updates on service issues, businesses must prioritize clear and concise communication channels that empower customers to feel heard and valued.

Empowerment and Autonomy

Empowering frontline employees with the autonomy to make decisions and take ownership of customer interactions is instrumental in cultivating a People-First culture. By equipping employees with the authority to resolve issues promptly and creatively, businesses empower them to deliver personalized and responsive service that exceeds customer expectations. This not only enhances employee morale but also fosters a culture of accountability and continuous improvement.

Going Above and Beyond

Exceptional customer service often lies in the willingness to go beyond—surpassing expectations and creating memorable experiences that leave an impression. Whether it's providing personalized recommendations, offering unexpected benefits, or resolving issues with empathy and grace, businesses that prioritize a People-First Attitude differentiate themselves by their unwavering commitment to customer satisfaction.

Example: Zappos

Zappos, the renowned online shoe retailer, epitomizes the People-First approach to customer service. Beyond its legendary commitment to free shipping and hassle-free returns, Zappos distinguishes itself through its culture of empathy, empowerment, and personalized service. Customer service representatives are encouraged to prioritize empathy over metrics, spending as much time as needed to listen to customers' concerns and provide tailored solutions. This People-First ethos has earned Zappos a devoted following of loyal customers who value not just the products they purchase but the exceptional service experience that accompanies every interaction.

A People-First Attitude Conclusion

A People-First Attitude is not merely a strategy—it's a mindset, a philosophy, and a fundamental commitment to treating customers as valued individuals rather than transactions. By understanding customer needs, fostering responsive communication, empowering employees, and going beyond expectations, businesses can cultivate a culture of customer-centricity that sets them apart in a crowded marketplace. In embracing the principles of a People-First Attitude, businesses not only enhance customer satisfaction and loyalty but also forge enduring relationships that transcend mere transactions, fostering a legacy of trust, authenticity, and mutual respect.

Technical and Critical Problem-Solving Skills—Navigating the Digital Landscape

In today's digital age, mastering technical and critical problem-solving skills is indispensable for delivering seamless and efficient customer service experiences. From troubleshooting technical issues to resolving complex inquiries, proficiency in digital tools and problem-solving methodologies is essential. Let's delve deeper into how businesses can approach this aspect practically:

Continuous Training and Development

Investing in continuous training and development programs is crucial for equipping customer service representatives with the technical skills needed to navigate the digital landscape effectively. This includes providing comprehensive training on the organization's digital platforms, customer relationship management (CRM) systems, communication tools, and troubleshooting techniques. Regular updates and refresher courses ensure that employees remain abreast of the latest technological advancements and best practices.

Resourceful Problem-Solving

Encouraging resourceful problem-solving is essential for empowering employees to tackle complex issues independently. Rather than relying solely on predefined solutions or scripts, customer service representatives should be encouraged to think critically, explore alternative approaches, and leverage available resources to resolve customer inquiries creatively. This may involve accessing knowledge bases, collaborating with cross-functional teams, or leveraging automation tools to streamline processes and expedite resolutions.

Digital Literacy and Adaptability

Fostering digital literacy and adaptability is essential for navigating the ever-evolving digital landscape effectively. Customer service representatives should possess a foundational understanding of digital technologies, including web browsers, mobile applications, social media platforms, and cloud-based solutions. Additionally, they should demonstrate agility and adaptability in learning new tools and methodologies as technology continues to evolve. This may involve providing access to online learning resources, workshops, and certification programs to enhance digital fluency and confidence.

Data-Driven Decision-Making

Empowering customer service representatives with data-driven decision-making skills is instrumental in optimizing service delivery and enhancing customer satisfaction. By leveraging analytics tools and customer feedback data, representatives can gain valuable insights into customer behaviors, preferences, and pain points. This enables them to identify trends, anticipate needs, and personalize interactions to meet individual customer requirements effectively. Additionally, data-driven insights can inform strategic initiatives and process improvements, driving continuous innovation and enhancement of the customer service experience.

Example: Amazon

Amazon's customer service prowess is grounded in its mastery of digital technology and data analytics. Customer service representatives are equipped with sophisticated tools and dashboards that provide real-time access to customer data, order history, and product information. By leveraging predictive analytics and machine learning algorithms, representatives can anticipate customer needs, proactively address potential issues, and personalize recommendations based on past behavior. This data-driven approach not only enhances efficiency and responsiveness but also fosters a culture of continuous improvement and innovation within the customer service organization.

A Technical and Critical Problem-Solving Skills Conclusion

In navigating the digital landscape, mastering technical and critical problem-solving skills is paramount for delivering exceptional customer service experiences. By investing in continuous training and development, encouraging resourceful problem-solving, fostering digital literacy and adaptability, and embracing data-driven decision-making, businesses can equip their customer service representatives with the tools and techniques needed to excel in the digital age. In doing so, they not only enhance efficiency and effectiveness but also elevate the overall customer service experience, fostering long-term loyalty and advocacy among customers.

Personal and Professional Skills—Building Trusted Relationships

In the dynamic landscape of customer service, building trust and fostering authentic relationships is paramount for driving customer satisfaction, loyalty, and retention. Personal and professional skills play a pivotal role in this endeavor, encompassing a wide range of competencies—from active listening and empathy to conflict resolution and cultural competence. Let's explore how businesses can approach this aspect practically:

Empathy and Active Listening

Empathy lies at the heart of meaningful customer interactions. Customer service representatives should demonstrate genuine empathy by actively listening to customers, acknowledging their emotions, and validating their concerns. This involves practicing active listening techniques such as paraphrasing, summarizing, and asking clarifying questions to ensure a deep understanding of customers' needs and emotions. By demonstrating empathy, representatives can establish rapport, build trust, and foster authentic connections with customers.

Effective Communication

Effective communication is essential for building trust and fostering positive relationships with customers. Customer service representatives should communicate clearly, confidently, and respectfully, using language that is easily understood and free of jargon. This includes active listening, asking open-ended questions, and providing clear and concise explanations or instructions. Additionally, representatives should demonstrate professionalism and courtesy in all interactions, maintaining a positive and solution-oriented demeanor even in challenging situations.

Conflict Resolution and Problem-Solving

Conflict resolution skills are invaluable for navigating challenging customer interactions and resolving disputes effectively. Customer service representatives should approach conflicts with patience, empathy, and diplomacy, seeking to understand the root cause of the issue and collaborating with customers to find mutually acceptable solutions. This may involve de-escalating tense situations, managing expectations, and negotiating compromises that balance customer satisfaction with business objectives. By demonstrating empathy and flexibility, representatives can turn potentially negative experiences into opportunities to strengthen trust and loyalty.

Cultural Competence

In a diverse and multicultural society, cultural competence is essential for building rapport and connecting with customers from different backgrounds and perspectives. Customer service representatives should strive to understand and respect cultural norms, values, and communication styles, adapting their approach accordingly to ensure inclusivity and sensitivity. This may involve learning about customers' cultural backgrounds, greeting them in their native language, and avoiding assumptions or stereotypes that may inadvertently offend or alienate. By embracing cultural competence, representatives can foster a sense of belonging and trust among diverse customer populations.

Example: Ritz-Carlton

The Ritz-Carlton Hotel Company sets the gold standard for personalized customer service, embodying the ethos of "Ladies and Gentlemen serving Ladies and Gentlemen." Central to the Ritz-Carlton experience is a commitment to building trust and fostering authentic relationships with guests. Customer service representatives undergo extensive training in empathy, communication, and conflict resolution, empowering them to anticipate guests' needs, exceed their expectations, and resolve issues with grace and professionalism. By embodying the values of respect, integrity, and excellence, representatives cultivate enduring relationships built on trust, loyalty, and mutual respect.

A Personal and Professional Skills Conclusion

In the pursuit of exceptional customer service, personal and professional skills are indispensable for building trust, fostering authentic relationships, and driving customer satisfaction and loyalty. By cultivating empathy, practicing effective communication, honing conflict resolution skills, and embracing cultural competence, businesses can empower their customer service representatives to connect with customers on a deeper level, anticipate their needs, and deliver personalized experiences that resonate and endure. In doing so, they not only enhance the customer service experience but also strengthen the bonds of trust and loyalty that underpin enduring customer relationships.

The Consequences of Neglecting the Customer Service Experience

The consequences of not adhering to the three guidelines of customer service experience management—namely, a People-First Attitude, Technical and Critical Problem-Solving Skills, and Personal and Professional Skills—can be significant and far-reaching. Here's how each aspect, when neglected, can impact businesses and strategies to guard against such pitfalls:

1. **Neglecting a People-First Attitude**

   <u>Consequences</u>

   Without prioritizing customers' needs and emotions, businesses risk alienating customers, eroding trust, and damaging their reputation. Poor customer service experiences can lead to negative word-of-mouth, decreased customer loyalty, and ultimately, loss of revenue.

   <u>Guarding Against It</u>

   Businesses can guard against neglecting a People-First Attitude by instilling a customer-centric culture from top to bottom. This involves providing comprehensive training on empathy and communication skills, empowering employees to prioritize customer satisfaction over metrics, and soliciting regular feedback from customers to identify areas for improvement.

2. **Lacking Technical and Critical Problem-Solving Skills**

   <u>Consequences</u>

   Inadequate technical proficiency and problem-solving skills can result in inefficient service delivery, prolonged resolution times, and frustration for both customers and employees. This can lead to increased customer churn, decreased productivity, and loss of competitive advantage.

   <u>Guarding Against It</u>

   To guard against lacking technical and critical problem-solving skills, businesses should invest in continuous training and development programs that equip employees with the knowledge and tools needed to navigate the digital landscape effectively. This includes providing access to relevant resources, encouraging cross-functional collaboration, and fostering a culture of innovation and continuous learning.

3. **Overlooking Personal and Professional Skills**

   <u>Consequences</u>

   Ignoring the importance of personal and professional skills can result in strained customer relationships, increased conflict, and decreased employee morale. Without effective communication, empathy, and conflict resolution skills, businesses risk escalating minor issues into major disputes, tarnishing their brand image, and losing valuable talent.

<u>Guarding Against It</u>
To guard against overlooking personal and professional skills, businesses should prioritize hiring candidates with strong interpersonal skills and providing ongoing training and support to enhance these competencies. This includes offering workshops, coaching sessions, and role-playing exercises to help employees develop effective communication, empathy, and conflict resolution skills.

By proactively addressing these potential pitfalls and adhering to the three guidelines of customer service experience management, businesses can safeguard against the negative consequences of neglecting the customer service experience. Through a commitment to customer-centricity, technical proficiency, and personal and professional development, businesses can cultivate a culture of excellence that fosters loyalty, drives satisfaction, and ensures long-term success in the marketplace.

Conclusion—Elevating the Customer Service Experience

In the ever-evolving landscape of customer experience management, delivering on the promise of exceptional customer service is both an art and a science—a delicate balance of technical proficiency, interpersonal finesse, and unwavering commitment to customer-centricity. By embracing a People-First Attitude, mastering Technical and Critical Problem-Solving Skills, and honing Personal and Professional Skills, businesses can elevate the customer service experience from a transactional interaction to a transformative journey. As we navigate the complexities of the digital age, let us remain steadfast in our dedication to putting customers at the center, solving their problems with agility and empathy, and nurturing enduring relationships built on trust and authenticity. In doing so, we not only safeguard the loyalty of our customers but lay the foundation for sustainable growth and prosperity in the ever-evolving marketplace.

Chapter 5—The Net Promoter System (NPS) Done Right

Jim Bass, CCXP

"NPS creates a view of customer loyalty. The absolute score is less important than the trend. We learn from both Promoters and Detractors."

Jeff Immelt, CEO, General Electric

Introduction and Overview

Many companies track NPS (Net Promoter Score) as a key indicator of customer satisfaction, experience, and loyalty. Unfortunately, year after year many business leaders and employees find themselves questioning whether NPS is really making a difference to their customers, employees, and the business.

I think it's good practice to question or assess all survey programs, annually, or at least every 18 months. This forces businesses and teams to evaluate what is working and what is not working, and then adjust accordingly. This regular assessment also pushes teams and leaders to re-visit the goals or desired outcomes they hoped the program would achieve. Are the goals of the program the same or have they changed? Are the desired outcomes of the program being achieved? If not, why not? And conversely, if desired outcomes are being realized, then dig deeper to find out how and why, and then celebrate.

Why are businesses questioning NPS? The reasons for this disconnect are plentiful, but usually can be traced to a few root causes which usually result from lack of understanding, alignment, and support. We will dive deeper into these areas later in this chapter. The good news is that it's not too late to right-size your Net Promoter System and get on the fast track to reaping the rewards of customer and employee loyalty and engagement.

The content of this chapter is based on what I learned as a part of the NPS certification course and how I applied it working at several large, publicly held companies. When the Net Promoter System was used as an engagement tool, we were able to achieve a significant increase in the Net Promoter Score and improve products, services and relationships with customers, employees, and business partners.

In addition to explaining how NPS should be viewed and used, I will bring out many of the reasons companies do not realize the full benefits of NPS. I'll share some tried and true strategies which help businesses counteract the pitfalls of NPS and create a specific focus to drive results and outcomes from Net Promoter Systems. I will also give some suggestions on the types of performance targets and goals businesses should focus on instead of just the score.

I encourage everyone interested in Net Promoter Scores and Net Promoters Systems to learn more by reading **"The Ultimate Question 2.0"** by Fred Reichheld and Bain partner, Rob Markey. For those of you have "been there and done that," then look at Reichheld's follow-up book, **"Winning on Purpose: The Unbeatable Strategy of Loving Customers."** This book is another great resource, and I will refer to it a few times within this chapter. When we do the right things, the score will take care of itself.

"

Root Causes of Dissatisfaction With NPS

Let's get right to the important aspect. Many times, I have seen or heard where managers and leaders are told to implement NPS, and they just think it's another survey. They don't realize the critical importance, depth, and breadth of the Net Promoter System. To meet the implementation goal, they add the ultimate question to all their surveys and tag on an abbreviated closed-loop process. This creates a lot of effort and energy focused on the wrong aspect of NPS.

The main causes of dissatisfaction with NPS can be categorized into four areas.

- **Education/Expectations**: There is a lack of understanding about the goal of the system, what the system was designed to achieve, and how to leverage the Net Promoter System to achieve the business goals. The organization expects 100% of customer behaviors to match the score they gave (Promoter, Passive, Detractor), but this is an incorrect assumption. This lack of understanding makes the organization expect NPS to do much more than it was designed to do. Additionally, there is little education on the supporting closed-loop process. It becomes a checklist item for employees. They don't see the end-result or the value of the closed-loop activity. As a result, it becomes a low priority. Additionally, the lack of education creates an incorrect assumption that net promotion surveys should be applied to functional areas like installation, product, UX, support, service, etc.

- **Implementation**: The biggest downfall is implementing without understanding the how, why, and purpose of net promotion and how to leverage the Net Promoter System for success. It is usually implemented as a survey program with a lot of attention to score calculation and reporting. Many times, there is not enough planning and design for the audience of the survey, i.e., who are the decision makers, influencers, day-to-day users. As a result, they don't know how to apply feedback and insight. The closed-loop process is either non-existent, implemented with poorly defined goals, or not staffed properly. Eventually it becomes unsustainable for the organization.

- **Connection**: The rich verbatims and insight need to be connected to a Voice of the Customer (VoC) program. The survey operations team needs to include or connect the NPS survey activities into the overall quality process. Text analytics tools are extremely helpful to understand verbatims, but many times are an afterthought. NPS process and feedback should be connected to product, service, and sales teams and leaders. The goals of the Net Promoter System (not the score) need to be connected to business objectives and performance goals (more on this later in the chapter).

- **Organizational Alignment**: It starts from the top. Alignment of the goals and purpose of the Net Promoter System with the business goals and purpose must be explicit, clear, and simple. Without it, the pervasive thinking of NPS as a panacea metric or that it's the only metric needed to explain everything, will prevail and then everyone aligns around score-boarding. Leaders must be the role model for the right behaviors and be able to articulate the value of their organization's Net Promoter System.

Implementing with a clear understanding of the how, why, and purpose of net promotion and how to leverage the Net Promoter System is paramount. Clear measures of success must be defined, refined, and regularly reported.

Net Promoter System Versus Net Promoter Score

As part of the introduction of Fred Reichheld's **"Winning on Purpose"** he says:

> *"…the most resilient and sustainably successful firms consistently select one primary purpose: enrich the lives of their customers. Then they run their business accordingly."*

Reichheld mentions several times that when he was developing what we now call NPS, he was really trying to create a score he called *"Net Lives Enriched."* He was concerned that many businesses and leaders may see "Net Lives Enriched" as too soft and squishy, thereby making it unattractive to business leaders and executives. In his "Lead with Love" chapter in **"Winning on Purpose,"** Reichheld expresses he would like everyone to think of NPS as the *"Net Purpose Score"* which ties back to the purpose of enriching lives of customers.

At the highest level, a Net Promoter System is a set of processes (components) which:

- Gathers feedback from customers,
- Amplifies the voice of the Promoters,
- Engages Passives and non-responders,
- Transforms Detractors into trusted advisors,
- Drives improvements in products, services, and relationships.

Nested within the system is a closed-loop process or program which ensures the customer feels heard and knows what is being done with their feedback. Depending on the size and capability of the business, each one of the bullet points above could be its own program or process, with its own set of resources, tools, owners, and managers. Net Promoter Systems fail when there is no focus on the system components above. Rather than focusing on the score, businesses should focus on the *components* of the Net Promoter System and the business outcomes and metrics. Do the right things and the score will respond accordingly.

The Net Promoter Score is not a measure of effectiveness of the Net Promoter System.

Determining the effectiveness of a Net Promoter System really depends on what the business is hoping to achieve from implementing it. Most of the businesses where I worked or consulted had goals of increasing:

- New sales
- Add-on revenue
- Loyalty, i.e., contract renewals

If these are the goals, then the effectiveness of the Net Promoter System would be measured against those goals. The Net Promoter Score itself does not predict or guarantee sales or renewals. Businesses can have high scores and yet experience decreased revenues and renewals due to situations out of their control. On the other hand, businesses can have low scores and still realize increased sales and renewals.

The Net Promoter Score is a calculated number intended to be an *indicator* of customer loyalty. The score is an *indicator*, not a desired outcome; therefore, the score should not have the intense focus of the organization. Instead, keep a vigilant eye on sales, revenue, and renewal rather than the Net Promoter Score.

Here is a basic analogy to illustrate how businesses should view or use the Net Promoter Score to get the most out of a Net Promoter System. Think of the score as a gas gauge (or battery life indicator) in an automobile. Imagine you are driving your family to Disney World in Orlando, Florida. During the trip, how many times do you look at the fuel gauge? How long do you study the gauge each time? How much do you think about it after you look at it?

If you're like me, I just look at it briefly, just a few seconds, maybe once an hour. Based on what I see, I can make the decision to keep on driving at the same speed; or save fuel by slowing down or turning off the air conditioning; or I can start looking for a gasoline or charging station. The gauge helps me make an informed decision on the next steps of my journey, so I am able reach my destination safely and with minimal delay or discomfort for my passengers and me.

The fuel indicator tells me how much fuel (resource) I need and when it will be needed. It also informs whether I need to adjust the route I am driving, and whether I will make it on time to check into my hotel room, and whether I need to replan, make phone calls, etc. But again, it's just an indicator of one resource being utilized. I could still have a flat tire, traffic jam, engine lock-up, a rock to the window, a fender bender, etc., all of which could delay my journey, increase my costs, and decrease safety and comfort. Just like in business, there is not one single metric that can diagnose and predict how successful the business is or will be.

In this driving scenario, the mileage (number of fuel refills or charges) is not my goal; it's not my purpose or destination. I don't stop and analyze the gas gauge every time it moves. In business, though, many times, it seems we want to analyze every movement of the Net Promoter Score and draw attribution to something specific, a silver bullet, so the problem can be resolved. This drives CX teams and analysis teams crazy because, unfortunately, the score was not designed to be used this way. It's just an *indicator*; not a target, not a goal, not the holy grail, not a CX panacea, and certainly not intended to be sliced, diced, crunched, explained, and defended at every monthly and quarterly report-out.

Pitfalls of Net Promoter "Score-Boarding"
In the preface of Fred Reichheld's book, **"Winning on Purpose,"** he says.

> *"… too many practitioners are corrupting NPS by making the score the target than a measure that inspires learning and growth."*

NPS is a classic example of a stretched concept, pulled out of shape by overuse and misuse. Companies who are not realizing the value of a Net Promoter System have probably fallen into the pit of what I call "score boarding." When this happens:
- Chasing the score becomes the focus,
- Score-based behaviors become more important than customer-centric behaviors,
- Misunderstanding leads to misuse,
- Leveraging the Net Promoter System is replaced with score growth strategies.

Many businesses who are not achieving desired business results after implementing NPS have usually lost their way because of a shift of focus from customer listening and engagement, to "score-boarding." In other words, sending surveys and quickly focusing resources on score reporting and trending rather than on understanding what the customers are saying and then acting on that valuable feedback.

The Net Promoter System is much more than a number or a score. When the score becomes the focus of the organization, they lose sight of the improvement and engagement opportunities it brings. These are the foundations of loyalty.

Companies who focus on the score tend to put a lot of attention on making the Detractors happy in the short-term. The closed-loop process for Detractors becomes an escalation management activity. And let's face it: many executives, directors and managers have become valuable to their organizations because they are skilled at escalation management and putting out fires. Eventually, they are rewarded for doing a great job at saving customers. This becomes their comfort zone because it can be the most common way they receive accolades from their managers. Over time, putting out fires and saving accounts becomes the thing that makes them valuable to the organization. A shift away from score-boarding and escalation management toward focusing on the Net Promoter System can be scary because it goes against everything they were taught.

The problem with making the score the goal is that the score or number becomes the focus. It's human nature. We can't help it. As soon as executives find a KPI that could be tied to growth or revenue, it becomes the solution and the whole organization becomes focused on it—the number, the score. Following quickly behind come the incentive plans and rewards programs to improve the score. Performance objectives have a target score. Complex reporting and dashboards emerge. Everyone is watching the score to make sure they get their bonus or can keep their jobs.

As this shift to score boarding happens, the organization's focus is no longer on the customer, their voice, and their verbatims. Instead, the focus shifts to the natural comfort zone of business performance. Teams and departments develop their own targets, goals and processes designed to keep managers and individual contributors focused on increasing the score.

At this point, the score is no longer being used as an indicator, a gauge, a guide, or a signal—it has become the goal—and this one act renders the Net Promoter System ineffective. The score-boarding activities and their supporting tools, processes and reports overshadow the desired outcomes of increased loyalty and revenues, and improved products, service, and relationships.

Eventually, Net Promoter Score becomes a beast that must be fed and cared for every day. Just think of how much energy and resource goes into score-boarding just to receive no material result. What if all that effort and energy for score-boarding and slicing and dicing was allocated to the components of the Net Promoter System? Answer: the score would take care of itself. The score would become an indicator and would no longer be the holy grail. Relationships with customers and employees would improve. This improvement drives better business performance. Better performance translates to improved profits.

Use the Tool the Right Way

Fred Reichheld says, in the preface of his book **"Winning on Purpose,"**

> *"… while I am pleased that so many companies have embraced NPS, I am deeply troubled how badly most of them are implementing it—achieving only a tiny fraction of the system's potential impact."*

Mature Net Promoter Systems do more than predict loyalty, they cultivate it. How do they do it? There is organizational alignment and a shared understanding that:

- Customer-facing roles create Promoters.
- Business must deliver improvements to products and services.
- Business must structure itself to meet customer needs.
- Customer-centric cultures happen when the leaders and employees focus on customer success rather than business performance.
- Effort has a strong indirect correlation to loyalty.

In most situations where you're trying to solve a problem, knowing which tool to use is important. For example: you wouldn't try to chop down a tree with hedge-clippers or try to water your garden with a shovel. Similarly, once the right tool is selected, like an axe to chop down a tree, the tool must be used the right way to achieve the desired result.

For an axe to be effective at chopping down a tree:

- The blade must be sharpened.
- The handle must be held in a certain way so the blade can be leveraged.
- The blade must be targeted to a specific location.
- The handle must be wielded with strength in such a way that the blade starts to break down the tree.

The Net Promoter System is not just *any* tool… it's an *<u>engagement</u>* tool. When you use it the right way and combine it with regular communications to your customers and employees, it creates a powerful attraction. This attraction engages customers and employees. The power of this attraction makes Passives become Promoters. It causes non-respondents to re-engage and be willing to become Promoters. And when Promoters become reference customers, they bring in more business and more Promoters. Detractors will either become your trusted advisors or they will move on.

Reichheld also presents compelling examples of how a robust, closed-loop process combined with thoughtful action and communication can be an incredible engagement tool for customers, employees, and businesses. When customers and employees are engaged with each other and the business, positive energy becomes a catalyst for fundamental change. As a result, true partnerships start to emerge; clients start to recommend, refer, and promote the business, products, and services. Loyalty blooms.

How does this look in practice? This diagram below shows how to focus on the components of a Net Promoter System as well as a few examples of measures, metrics, objectives, and goals which drive engagement and shifts business attention away from the score and onto the Net Promoter System. It's all about doing the right things and letting the "number" take care of itself.

The right things from a Net Promoter System perspective are:

- Putting the Promoters to work and **amplifying** their voices.
- **Engaging** the Passives—they just need a reason to be a Promoter, so give it to them!
- Reaching out to and **re-committing** to the non-responders (they are the biggest risk).
- **Transform** the Detractors into trusted advisors.
- Implement **improvement** plans.
- **Simplify** business processes and infrastructures.

Measurements drive behaviors, so brainstorm measures that drive behaviors which:

- Engage, activate, secure Promoters
- Engage, convert Passives to Promoters
- Transform Detractors to Trusted Advisors
- Re-commit to Non-Responders (they are the greatest risk to attrition)
- Foster a customer-centric culture
- Improve employee and customer engagement

Let's take a closer look at why it's important to focus on these areas rather than the score.

Promoters beget Promoters. The power of a Net Promoter System is putting your Promoters to work. Goal setting in this area should be focused on creating the programs and platforms that put Promoters to work. You see some of the examples here like increasing reference accounts, testimonials, and videos and blogs. Another approach to amplifying their voice is to implement an advocacy platform. The new customers Promoters bring also tend to be Promoters as well.

Passives want to be Promoters. Give them a reason to be a Promoter by engaging with them. This is the low-hanging fruit. Show them on a regular basis that you are listening and acting on their feedback, and they will become Promoters. Goal setting in this area should be around the volume and frequency of communications; you should also create a conversion target, like convert 30% of Passives to Promoters. The goal you select may be lower or higher depending on the volume and needs of the organization.

Detractors want to see their improvement suggestions implemented. Depending on the number of Detractors, you may need to be strategic on who you focus on first. Communicate with them frequently so they know you are engaged, listening, and acting. Approach them with the goal of making them become your *trusted advisors*. Over time, show them how products and services are improving based on their feedback. As with Passives, business goals should contain a communication aspect as well as a conversion or transformation target.

Non-Responders are the greatest risk of attrition. Unlike Detractors, Non-Responders are not engaged enough to engage in and submit a survey. They are waiting for that proverbial "last straw" and have your competitor in mind. But if they see you acting on their feedback and engaging with your customer base to create improvement, they will be *attracted* and will entertain the idea of staying. They know the cost of switching to a competitor. When they see you acting, a financial conversation happens in their heads. They know it's cheaper and easier to stay with you. Engage with them as though they are a trusted advisor to your business. When they see you are taking customer feedback seriously, they trust their voices will be heard too. It's a win! Critical goals here are to communicate regularly so that they see what you are doing to improve, but also include a personal outreach and a recommit goal to a strategic group.

Improved products and services create value for customers and employees and lowers costs. Be sure the business has an appetite to deliver improvements and how much. Also, let the customers help validate what you've heard them say. Invite them to help prioritize what is delivered. Business goals should contain the implementation of an improvement plan, opportunities for customer prioritization and validation, and again a goal for regular communications.

Simplifying business processes and structure drives out customer effort. Look for ways to simplify internal and external processes throughout the organization. Being easy to do business with and providing a simple work environment is the foundation for employee and customer satisfaction and loyalty. Low effort has also been proven to be strongly correlated with loyalty. High effort creates disloyalty, while low effort creates loyalty. Find ways to talk in simple language. Get rid of technical-speak, corporate terms, and acronym language. Be easy, human, and plain in the way you speak and communicate. Business goals include creating or executing a business simplification strategy. Be sure it's part of the internal external communication strategy as well.

In summary, businesses cultivate loyalty by focusing energy on customer and employee engagement. When Net Promoter Systems are used correctly, a powerful engagement tool emerges. Regular communication expressing a sincere desire and ability to listen, learn, act, and improve is an intoxicating attractant which captures attention and creates engagement. The result is an engaged customer base and workforce, both of which translate into loyalty and lower marketing and attrition costs. As the culture in your organization transforms into one of "listening and taking action," the score-focused behaviors will be replaced with improvement-focused actions.

NPS Methodology Pitfalls

We are all human and subject to our own curiosity and need to measure up. Be mindful of these very tempting pitfalls which will corrupt your Net Promoter System and create frustration with employees and customers.

- **Comparing scores.** When companies focus on the score, they eventually want to compare their score to other businesses. This is difficult to do because most companies (especially publicly held companies) hold these numbers close to the vest. Because the score can be "gamed," no one wants to report a great score only to have the competition report a better score. On the other hand, no one wants to report a low score as it could impact stock prices or create mass dissatisfaction across the customer base. Also, a low score for one industry could be a high score for another. For example, with banking, 34 is a low score but would be exceptional for telecom.
- **Asking the ultimate question in every survey.** The ultimate question should not be asked on every interaction, transaction, product survey, UX survey, etc. Net Promotion does not translate well for transactional surveys and non-relationship surveys. Many times, the people who are responding to these kinds of surveys are not decision makers for the company. Additionally, the score calculation does not help the business understand how satisfied the customers are. The best practice is to ask questions about satisfaction, effort, and experience and to use a Top Box calculation or an index calculation.
- **Asking the ultimate question too often.** NPS is best suited for an annual relationship survey. Resist the temptation to send relationship surveys every quarter or every six months. This creates survey fatigue. And if the business is not making significant improvements every quarter or every six months, customers will become frustrated and opt out of the survey or they will simply stop responding. Don't keep asking the same question when no action has been taken to fully resolve ongoing issues which impact loyalty, satisfaction, and effort.
- **Surveying every user, manager, director, and leader.** Spend considerable time and effort to define your target audience. Know the roles of the responders and categorize them and their survey responses so the scores and insights can be sliced and diced by decision maker, influencer, advocate, user, etc. Businesses who want to know, manage, and mitigate the risk for loyalty should focus on the *decision makers*. These are the C-Suite or SVPs who have the complete authority to make the decision to continue buying from you or make the switch to a competitor. Directors, managers, and daily users don't have this power. The scores of these responder segments can be vastly different. End users may hate the product or relationship, but at the same time the decision makers may love the product or relationship because it adds value to the company and profit to the bottom line. Conversely, the decision makers may have an exceptionally low score because of business decisions they are making while end users are super happy with the company. Companies who aggregate the scores and insights from all responders may have a false sense of security, or they may think the sky is falling when in reality everything is okay.

Getting Back on Track With NPS

The Net Promoter System provides a measurement framework which helps business improve customer and employee experience, loyalty, engagement, and satisfaction. If your business has become disillusioned with NPS, found it complicated and unwieldy; or if it has become a distraction to employees and leaders; or if it is not yielding the value originally envisioned when it was implemented, take heart—you can get NPS back on track.

- Re-visit the goals and business outcomes you want to achieve and document them.
- Educate leaders on the capabilities of a Net Promoter System, how to leverage it, how to use it the right way, and how to avoid pitfalls and what "not" to do.
- Remove the score from business objectives and goals. This will prevent score-based behaviors and will help everyone within the organization focus on activities and programs which drive customer-centric behaviors.
- Instead of driving the organization to a score, identify measures and metrics which support the Net Promoter System components and make them the target or goal. **Do the right things and the score will reflect the great things you are doing.**
- Assess the current survey program and voice of the customer program; update and align them.
- Activate teams and departments to amplify the voice of the Promoters; develop an advocacy program and connect it to the Net Promoter System and goals.
- Activate and empower teams to engage Passives and non-responders.
- Develop a team to transform Detractors into trusted advisors.
- Communicate with customers and employees what you are learning from them via the Net Promoter System.
- Leverage customer and product advisory boards to help validate and prioritize improvements.

Final Thoughts

All of us want to manage and run our businesses in a way that empowers employees, provides value to customers, and at the same time yield profits which sustain the company, the customers, and the employees. To accomplish this in the 21st century is no easy feat. There are so many ways leaders can become distracted. If NPS is a distraction from creating value for employees and customers, then wise leaders must take a step back and revisit the reason for implementing it in the first place.

NPS is so much more than a score, a survey, or a process. It's a framework which allows us to lead with love. Fred Reichheld mentions _"Leading with Love"_ throughout his book, **"Winning on Purpose"** and this is what true NPS is all about. He gives four bullet points to keep leaders on track. Since he says it much more wisely and succinctly than I ever could, I am including them here.

1. "Function as a role model for the right behaviors and explain major decisions and priorities in terms of core values."
2. "Foster a culture that embraces playing the long game, ensuring that short-term financial goals never trump principles."
3. "Make the customer the center of every decision—from product development to employee hiring to digitizing customer service and operations."
4. "Break down barriers (organizational and other) that impede progress."

Chapter 6—Data Inventories for Better Experiences

Gary C. David

> *"You can have data without information, but you cannot have information without data".*
> **Daniel Keys Moran**

The Futility of Point-of-Sale Surveys: A Customer's Perspective

We all know the moment. All you want to do is pay for whatever it is you are buying and then leave the store. But before you can complete your transaction, the cashier prompts you to take that extra step. "Can you please respond to the question on the keypad using the numbers provided?" The question is typically about whether we "enjoyed our experience" while shopping at the store, in which we may have only spent five minutes. Most people wouldn't even consider the time spent in the store as an experience.

You could argue that in the most technical sense it was an "experience." After all, isn't everything on some level an experience? At the same time, was it so much of an experience that it requires you to use a keypad and rate how good or bad it was. Sure, I'll give you a "9", which is the highest score since that is the highest number on the keypad (you can't combine the 1 and 0). Why did I give it a 9? No reason. Probably I just didn't want the person working at the counter to get hassled by a manager who is going to want to talk to them about how much more effort they could be putting into their minimum wage service sector job.

The Need for Comprehensive Data Strategies

As a researcher, I know that the "survey" I was given really has no validity or reliability. The question itself does not capture the complexity of what constitutes an "experience," nor delves into how I perceived it. Thus, the results of the survey are meaningless from a statistical standpoint. As an experienced designer, however, I know companies treat this data as meaningful, and make the data matter. In other words, the metric only matters because people have decided that it matters.

Customer experience, like all businesses, is driven by data. A problem lies, however, in defining what we mean by data. We can become too accustomed to certain kinds of data and data collection to the exclusion to others, resulting in data blind spots that need to be remedied if we are to better understand the experience we are designing and the impact those designs are having.

For companies and customer experience professionals, it is important to have a multi-methodological data strategy to fully understand the experiences that customers are having. This chapter will introduce you to a Data Inventory, meant to not only help you think critically about the data you are collecting and identify gaps, but also think strategically about data and data collection to create and evaluate experiences.

Understanding Data

At an amazingly simple level, data is just a collection of material or things that is meant as a representation of something that we are interested in understanding. *Any object or thing can become data when it is used to try to further our understanding of a situation*. What turns something into data is that it is viewed as data. The temperature outside is just "the temperature" until it is viewed as representational of something else more significant. The temperature might be part of a trend, a sign of something else (like global warming), an indication of what we should wear that day, confirming the accuracy of a forecast, and many other things. In the eyes of someone trying to perform an analysis, temperature becomes data. In the eyes of everyone else, it is just temperature. What this means is that anything has the potential to be data if we view it as part of a purposeful analysis. Or, to put it differently, *what makes something 'data' is that we look at it as data.*

When people talk about "data," they are most often referring to numbers or quantitative data. But not all numbers represent the same types of things. The primary distinction is what can be called *metrics* versus *indicators*. A metric is something that refers to a discrete quantity that is objectively measurable. Simple examples of this would be weight, height, volume, area, number of calls taken, length of wait time on hold, inventory, etc. The point here is that the metric is not up for debate. At the same time, the metrics do not necessarily mean anything in and of themselves.

Indicators are what data shows us, or 'indicates.' As we discussed, temperature as a metric only tells us what the temperature is at that moment. What that temperature indicates is another matter altogether. Indicators get to interpretation and discerning what the data could mean. This ultimately means that to make data meaningful, there must be a certain level of interpretation. Even though people associate interpretation with qualitative (non-numeric) data, interpretation is part of any kind of data analysis. The data rarely, if ever, speaks for itself. Rather, data typically must be spoken for regarding what it means and what action should be taken because of it.

Data by itself doesn't mean much of anything. If I told you I was driving 65 miles per hour, all that it shows is that I was driving at a particular rate of speed. But what does that mean? I could be following the speed limit (a good thing) but doing so in the left lane of the expressway (an annoying thing). I could be driving that fast on a surface street (an illegal thing), or even in a neighborhood subdivision street (an irresponsible and dangerous thing). I might be doing 65 mph in reverse across a lawn (a bad but kind of impressive thing). To make sense of any data, we need to add *context*. Put another way, I like to think of the following equation:

Data + Context = Information

Data by itself is not information; it becomes information by adding context. Context is the framework through which data can be viewed and evaluated. We can think of the proverbial glass that is filled up halfway. How we evaluate it depends on how we view it, or the perspective that we take. Different perspectives and different frameworks can lead to different interpretations. For instance, the number of tickets handed out might be a good thing because it shows the police are focusing on public safety. It might be a bad thing because police are engaging in behavior that targets a particular community. We need to look at the data through different lenses to understand the different things that the data can indicate or mean as information.

This is one reason having different perspectives when evaluating data can be helpful because it can yield greater insights into what the data can mean. Different contexts can provide us with different information. In the end, different kinds of information can lead to different kinds of action. Therefore, having context becomes crucially important to our analysis of data. And when it comes to understanding context, the more and different types of data, the better.

Triangulating Context

Triangulation is a concept that is most frequently used when finding a position on a map. When triangulating, we can use two fixed positions to determine the location of something. Additionally, we can use three positions, like police and emergency services can use cell phone towers, to find the position of someone in need. The goal is to find our position so that we know where we are, and how to get to where we want to go.

In data analysis, we also speak of triangulation to have greater understanding of what we are trying to research and greater confidence in our findings. Here, triangulation involves using multiple types of data collection approaches which provide a range of types of data. Triangulation is often used as an approach in qualitative research but extends as a strategy in quantitative research as well. Again, the goal is to have greater confidence in our research and our findings, which then will lead to greater confidence in the decisions we make based on those findings.

In this way, triangulation reminds me of a lesson from rock climbing. There are times when doing multi-pitch rock climbing that you need to set a solid anchor at a fixed point. This is done using stable natural features (if available) or using artificial temporary anchors (known as 'protection) that you use in conjunction with the rock wall. When setting anchors, the rule was to set three anchor points if possible and at least two in a pinch. Unless an anchor was "bomb proof" (i.e., would not fail under load), you needed to set up multiple points to limit the chance of falling through anchor failure. Additionally, you needed to connect the anchors in such a way that the load was distributed evenly to reduce the load on any of them, increasing their overall strength and stability. The same idea can be applied to data collection and analysis.

Let's look at an example that people might be able to relate to. Attrition rate, or the loss of employees at a company, is a metric. We can see how many employees left a company over a particular time as a verifiable fact. As a metric, though, it doesn't really tell us much as it cumulatively counts all attrition whether voluntary or involuntary. Let's say we are going to focus on voluntary attrition, or those who left the company by their own choice. People might decide to leave because they do not like working at the company because of the organizational culture (a bad thing). However, people might leave the company because they received such good professional development that they found better opportunities outside the organization (a good thing). These people can become employee ambassadors, talking about how much they gained from working at the company and thereby resulting in it being a sought-after company (an incredibly good thing). One the other hand, if it is a bad culture, then they are going to be organizational detractors and tell people to avoid the organization (a bad thing).

The Importance of Context and Multi-Methodological Data in Customer Experience Metrics

We can take a customer experience example by looking at the metric "average handle time" which is the average time that it takes to fulfill customer's needs or request. AHT often is used as a KPI for call (or contact) centers, with the thinking that the shorter the time, the better the outcome. As a metric, it tells us what it is described as. But again, what does it mean or indicate? How does customer happiness or unhappiness correlate with AHT? What is happening on the calls that might give us better context and understanding of the calls? Is there a connection between length of handle time and customer churn? There are any number of questions that we could ask, and data that we could collect, which would provide us with a better context, and ultimately better information.

We cannot determine what the metric is an indicator of without additional context. We can gain that context through additional data in the same way that additional anchors while rock climbing provide greater security. There are any number of data sources that we could use, such as exit interviews, exit surveys, social media postings, conversations with managers, employee dashboards, feedback from employee resource groups, and so on. The more data we have, and the more perspectives we have on what that data means, the more confident we can be in our findings regarding why people are leaving.

Each data collection methodology has advantages and disadvantages, and it is important to be aware of those features when selecting what approaches we are going to be using. The data strategy we have should be based on a balancing of those advantages and disadvantages. Much like setting anchors while rock climbing, we want to have those methods balanced in terms of strengths and weaknesses, as well as redundancies. Having built in redundancies means that if one thing fails, then we are backed up by the others. Taken together, our data strategy should have a multi-methodological approach as a foundational feature, and make sure that we are able to triangulate our context so that we can have better analysis and ultimately sounder information upon which we can base our actions.

The Data Inventory

To create a better data strategy, I advocate for the use of a Data Inventory, which has us place our data collection approaches in the following 2x2 table shown below.

On the x axis, we show whether the data is descriptive or attitudinal. Descriptive refers to data and analysis that is more objective in that there is not interpretation of what the data means, but rather a focus on what the data provides in terms of details. This focus can be compared to attitudinal data, which is more subjective or perceptual.

On the y axis, we have the traditional breakdown of quantitative versus qualitative data. In their simplest form, quantitative refers to numeric data. Beyond that, we also can think about quantitative as structured data, built into readily identifiable packets that make it relatively manageable because it is in a standardized format which makes it more easily analyzed. Qualitative data, by comparison, is non-numeric. It is also unstructured in nature, meaning that it is harder to manage because we must give it structure through our analysis (such as in coding). Most often we think of this as words that are written or verbal, but also can include photographs, music, artwork, objects, or really anything else.

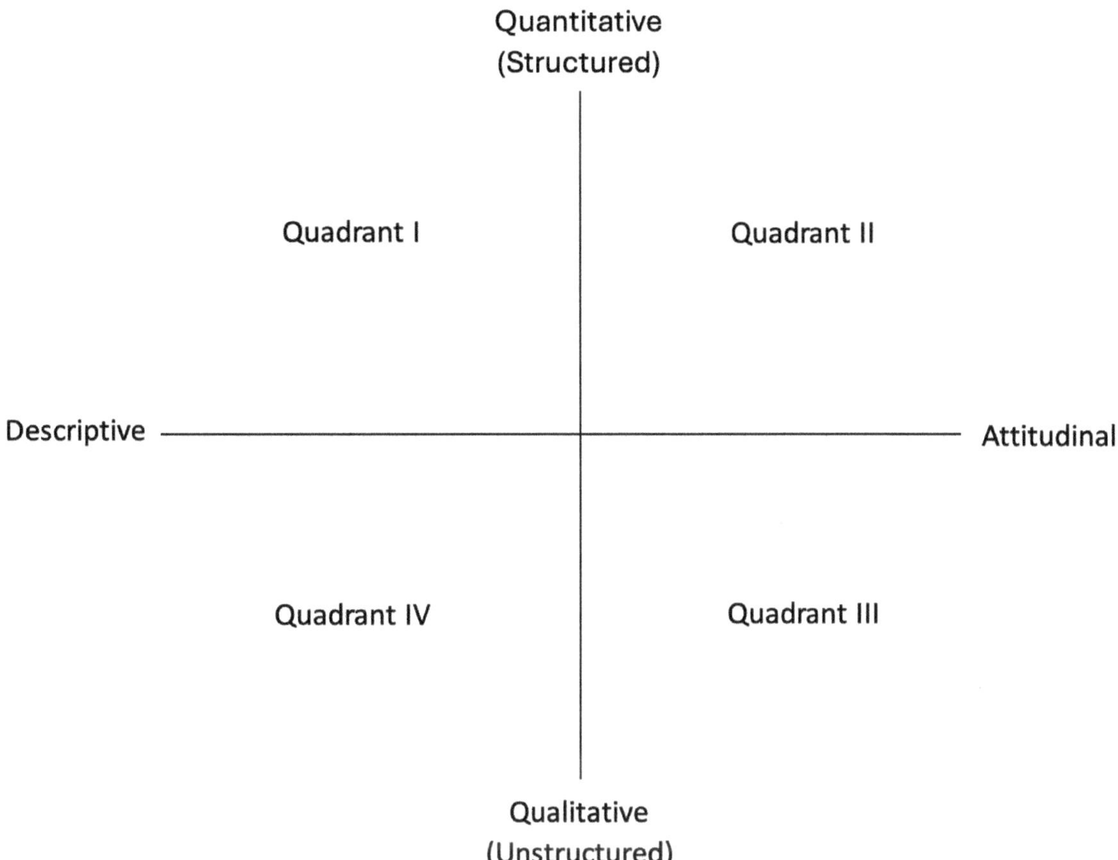

In Quadrant I, we can see data that is quantitative and descriptive. In its simplest form, we have numbers that describe quantities or are reflected in formulas. We previously discussed data like attrition rate or average handle time. We also might think of this quadrant trying to provide an understanding of what is occurring or exists as a metric (versus an indicator). Repeated measurements would yield the same results (if the measuring instrument is reliable) because we are trying capture something that is concrete and in essence non-debatable.

In Quadrant II, we are trying to capture people's attitudes by turning those attitudes into structured data. The simplest example of this is any Likert scale that asks people to turn their perceptions and thoughts into numeric values based on a scale that has been provided by the researcher. Net Promoter Score (NPS) is Quadrant II data in that it is asking about an attitudinal state (How *likely* are you to recommend…) versus an existent state (Have you *ever* recommended). When we turn something as complex as experiences into a number, then we are operating in Quadrant II.

In Quadrant III, we are still trying to capture attitudes, but are providing the opportunity to respond in an unstructured way. Typically, open-ended questions on a survey provide an opportunity for people to provide their attitudes and perceptions. Interviews and focus groups, assuming that people are allowed to answer in an unstructured manner, also fit in this quadrant. Increasingly, companies are looking at social media posts as a source of Quadrant III data. If we are doing observations in a field setting, the notes that we take also will be unstructured data. A key part of unstructured data is that the analysis relies in large part on the analyst's understanding of the data. In qualitative data analysis, the researcher is most inserted into the process in Quadrant III in terms of their judgement regarding what the data means.

Finally, Quadrant IV involves the analysis of unstructured data but in a descriptive, rather than interpretive, manner. For instance, I am trained in an approach called conversation analysis (CA). In CA, we try to describe the structures of talk as they occur in interactions. Thus, there is attention given to describing the features of the interaction (or *how* things are done) versus interpreting perceptions and causes of the interaction (or *why* things are done). We want to dive deeply into the details of the interactions, even going as far as to look at the length of pauses, where overlaps in talk occur, how certain words may be elongated or shortened, and even inbreaths and outbreaths. Again, a key feature of this is to limit any interpretation, but rather focus on description. Also, in terms of Quadrant IV we might describe the features of a room or setting, the arrangement of items and objects, the sound quality of something, or anything else that we are able to take in through our senses. Value is not placed on these descriptions. If we are thinking in terms of objectivity and subjectivity, the goal here is to be as objective, or value-neutral, as possible.

To perform a data inventory, we would not only want to think of the type of data that is collected, but also how that data is treated. For instance, I have seen the tendency to turn qualitative data into quantitative data. Speech analytics software has this tendency as it takes what is said during an interaction (qualitative data) and transforms it into numerical scores and representations (quantitative data). We always must provide some structure to data to make it useful through analysis, but over-structuring unstructured data can remove the proprieties that make it most valuable. Counting how many people are in a café can obscure the richness of the setting. Counting how many times a word is said during an interview or phone call can remove the context in which it occurs, as well as the deeper meaning behind it. We need to keep in mind that to turn data into information we need context.

The Data Inventory simply calls on you to place into the matrix what kind of data you are collecting and how you are analyzing it. You can also think about in what quadrant is your organization most reliant or greatest attention is given to. Most organizations are very quantitatively driven, which perhaps is understandable. There is the belief that by virtue of their numerical value, quantitative data is more objective and actionable. People (e.g., managers and decision makers) may feel that the "numbers speak for themselves," and therefore we don't have to decide; the decision is made for us by the numbers. In most business, there is something that I would call the Cult of the Quantitative, where numbers are worshipped as divine beings and oracles through which the future can be discerned and grace achieved.

However, as we have seen, numbers in themselves are not objective, and frequently do not speak for themselves. In fact, in any quantitative analytic approach, the final step is to always *interpret* the data. We must figure out what the results mean and how we can use them to guide action. As in our rock-climbing example, the goal of the Data Inventory is to create a more solid data anchor on which we can make more stable and strategic decisions. The inventory provides an opportunity to see where we might be too reliant on certain data, have gaps in other kinds of data, and see opportunities to improve.

Increasingly in academia, there is the expectation that researchers will employ multiple methodologies in their studies. It is hard to get federally funded grants without a data strategy that has different methodologies and types of data. The 'data wars' that pitted the quantitative versus the qualitative have long passed. Today, data collection and analysis techniques are viewed as tools in research toolbox from which the right tools for the right job are pulled. The Data Inventory is meant to make sure that we are using all the tools that we have at our disposal.

Putting the Data Inventory into Action

Experiences by their very nature are difficult to capture and understand. The nature of experiences has long been a focus philosophy going back millennia. It is too complex to reduce to one number based on one question. Such approaches are attractive because of their simplicity, and there is something to be said for simplicity. At the same time, such simplicity can mask the complexity at the heart of experiences. To capture this complexity, we need to have a fully evolved data strategy.

The goal of any research is to extend our understanding of a phenomena or topic. We not only want our results to be reliable and valid, but also trustworthy and authentic. By this I mean we want to be able to see the phenomena and topic reflected in the results in such a way that we trust the outcomes and action they inspire. The Data Inventory is meant to provide this sense through maturing our data strategy.

Any data collection and analysis process come down to execution at every step of the journey. Because we are researching and analyzing people, people are an inescapable part of the equation. Rather than seeing that as a limitation or liability, we can lean into that as an asset. Experiences are a rich part of our everyday lives. Understanding those experiences requires that we not lose that richness. Additionally, we need that richness to translate into actionable insights. The Data Inventory is one way to provide added context to diversified data which will lead to reliable information and ultimately strategic action and make us less reliant on scores that are generated from touchpads at checkout.

Chapter 7—The Art & Science of CX Storytelling: Techniques for Change and Connection

Judy Bloch

> *"The answer does not lie in data, but in the stories."*
>
> **Howard Schultz, former CEO of Starbucks**

Introduction to Storytelling in CX

Storytelling plays a critical role in human communications. From prehistoric humans drawings to parents reading stories to young children, to the latest viral Tik Tok, creative storytelling is a technique used throughout history to captivate and inspire. In fact, research indicates that 65% of daily conversations are grounded in storytelling.[1]

At its core, storytelling is both an art and a science, allowing us to create emotional and intelligent impact with our audience. As an art, storytelling is a creative process to weave together words, images, data, and examples to make an emotional connection with the audience. As a science, storytelling provides a consistent structure for what creates a good and, presumably, memorable story, allowing us to draw logical conclusions and inspire action. Poorly crafted stories can also be memorable, of course, although that may not be the impression we want to make on the audience!

As a Customer Experience (CX) leader, our primary goal is to inspire action and drive continuous improvement across the enterprise. We are constantly called upon to make presentations, lead workshops and spearhead initiatives. Just as we seek to make a connection between customers and our brand, as CX Leaders, we also need to be able to make a connection with our stakeholders to influence change within the organization.

CX leaders, that master storytelling, have at their disposal a powerful technique to leverage customer feedback and behavioral insights to inspire action and influence stakeholders. There are several different techniques and approaches to CX Storytelling in professional settings, including:

- **Personal anecdote**—Crafting and sharing stories that pull from your own, unique experience to illustrate a message or create empathy with the customer's experience. Creating a personal connection can help to establish credibility and inspire action.
- **Immersive/Experiential**—A technique that is designed to make audience members feel as though they are in the customer's shoes and as though they are there, experiencing what they did. This serves as a creative way to foster active engagement and participation from audience members.
- **Analytical**—Storytelling can make your data and insights more memorable. Using this technique to blend data with a narrative, and frequently visualizations, the facts presented become 22 times more likely to be remembered.[2]

---

1 https://www.scientificamerican.com/article/the-secrets-of-storytelling/

2 https://www.forbes.com/sites/kateharrison/2015/01/20/a-good-presentation-is-about-data-and-story/?sh=7813d8eb450f

- **Historical retelling/Crystal ball**—Retelling of actual customer events and occurrences help the audience connect with the impact and end outcome, like the approach taken by the 'Ghost of Christmas Past' in Charles Dickens' Scrooge. These stories can also be repositioned to help shape what could be, as seen with the 'Ghost of Christmas Future;' an approach that can help inspire action by planting seeds of fear and doubt.

Outcomes of CX Storytelling

CX Leaders often find themselves in a role where they must influence and inspire action, given they often don't have full ownership over the areas where improvements to the customer experience are necessary. This is where CX Storytelling comes in. CX Storytelling is frequently leveraged to help CX Leaders and Practitioners sell stakeholders on CX concepts, provide relevance to data, set context for policies, and create purpose beyond the action necessary.

CX Storytelling can be an immensely powerful tool to connect stakeholders with the 'why' behind customer experiences strategies and principles. For example, particularly in healthcare, it's common for leaders to start with their "connect to purpose" story. It's the reason they work in healthcare and is usually grounded in a story of themselves or their loved ones throughout a healthcare experience.

There are three primary outcomes, or intentions, behind choosing to leverage a CX Storytelling approach. Each option has unique goals and attributes that help CX Leaders achieve their desired outcome:

- **To Educate:** This is a common outcome when sharing customer stories to help organizations across the enterprise better understand the customer's experience. It is frequently used when collaborating with frontline teams and leadership to emphasize the reason behind a policy change or why a given guideline is important and the downstream impacts if not followed. Often a historical retelling or crystal ball approach is effective when the goal is to educate.
- **To Enlighten**: When striving to enlighten the audience, CX Leaders are typically looking to build empathy and establish a deeper understanding of the customer's journey and pain points. An analytical storytelling approach works well when building empathy. Personal anecdotes are a good fit when the goal is to enlighten.
- **To Motivate Change**: Studies confirm that decision making is often based on emotion and justified with logic.[3] Using CX Storytelling, leaders can create an emotional connection with decision makers and help influence the outcome. While personal anecdotes and analytical approaches can be successful, leveraging an immersive or experiential approach to storytelling can often catch an audience by surprise—in a good way—and help the CX Leader achieve their desired outcome.

---

3   https://medium.com/@salesforce/neuroscience-proves-we-buy-on-emotion-and-justify-with-logic-but-with-a-twist-4ff965cdeed8

3 SIMPLE WAYS TO

Leverage CX Storytelling

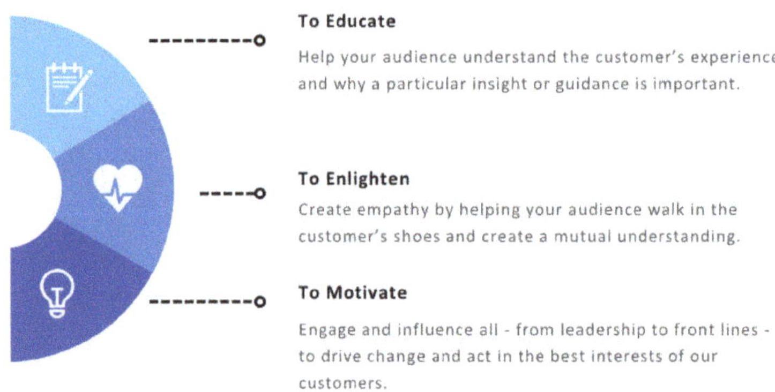

Case Study #1: Inspiring Action through Experiential Storytelling

To properly introduce and share an example of inspiring action through experiential CX storytelling, we first must set the stage. Imagine leading a digital CX team, whose goal is to contain customers within the digital channels—online and apps—and prevent customers from falling out to more experience servicing channels, i.e., the call center. The digital CX team is very tightly aligned with the agile development teams for each defined customer journey, with the CX analyst essentially serving as 'production quality control.'

The login CX analyst detected a change in customer behavior, indicating that login volume was significantly down. This change in customer behavior immediately followed a page redesign that moved the login button from the upper right, toward the bottom of the page and was driving calls with customers citing login issues. While the CX Analyst knew the unexpected customer behavior was due to the design change, IT had done their analysis and determined there were no technical issues. IT confirmed that the login success rate was as expected, which resulted in a stalemate of sorts in getting the customer pain point resolved.

During this issue investigation and analysis, it just so happened that a group of top senior executives would be touring the CX Command Center, where the analysts worked and collaborated with cross-functional teams. Knowing this audience well, the CX Leader took the opportunity to craft an interactive, theatrical presentation, complete with a script and acting roles, in which the Chief Operating Officer (COO) would sit down at a desk and be asked to log in to the platform—just as customers do every day. Naturally though, this mock up site had the login button hidden, below the fold and scrolling just happened to be disabled.

After listening to the team's presentation about all the great work being done at the Command Center, the executive sat down to login to the platform, and was of course unsuccessful. He was then asked what he would do next to solve his problem—the answer of course was to call the Contact Center and explain that he "was unable to login"—the exact same wording the call center agents were hearing.

The presentation wrapped up with the CX Leader quite literally passing a hat around to these senior leaders, asking them to sponsor an analyst so that we could expand our listening operations, find, and fix these types of experience issues across our full digital footprint. An unorthodox approach, certainly, but it worked.

Not only was the budget approved to grow the team, we also finally got resources and prioritization to resolve the login issue and move the button back to where customers expected it to be.

Finding your CX Story—Steps for Crafting Your Narrative

It's possible that the process of finding your CX story may be an iterative one, with multiple rounds of revisions and versions along the path to achieving your desired outcome. Following this 6-step process will ensure your story is well thought through and meets the unique considerations of your specific scenario.

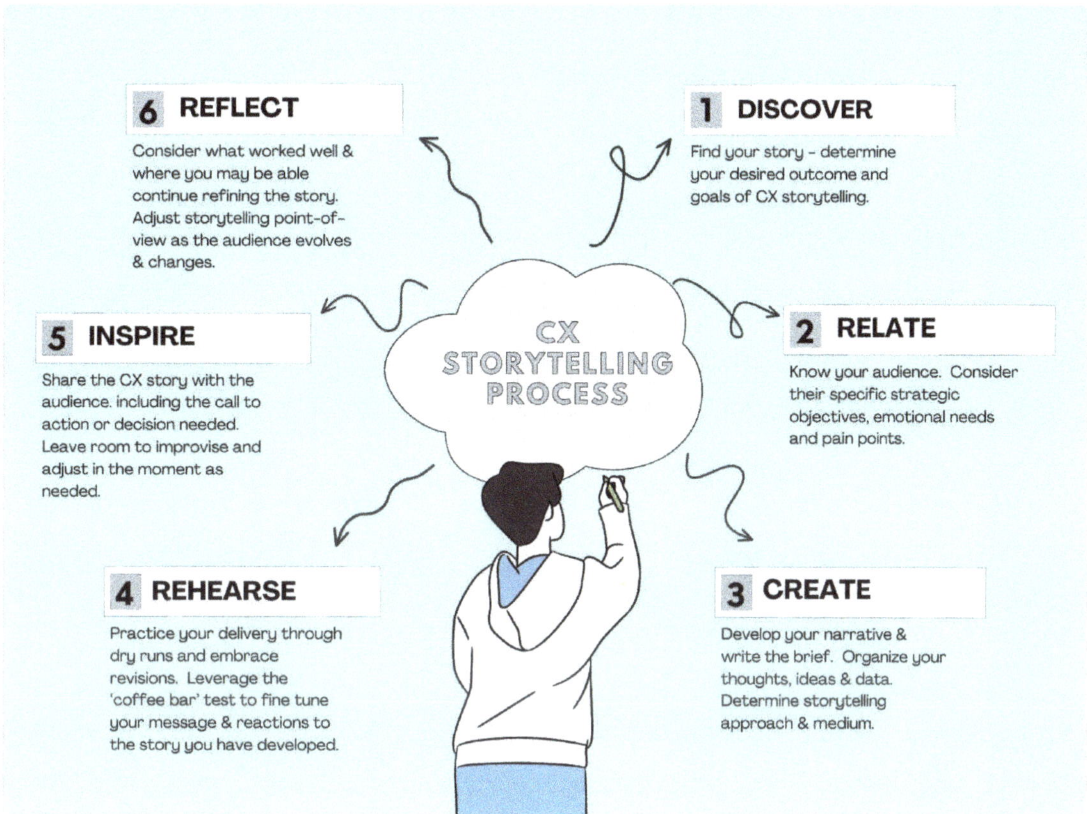

- **Step 1: Discover**. Focus on finding your story. Determine the singular focus of this story, knowing that this idea may change which version you tell. Are you trying to solve a problem? Do you want to sell an idea? Need to rally the troops? Explain a complex topic? Lock in on the idea you want to convey and desired outcome.
- **Step 2: Relate**. Get to know your audience and what's important to them. Seek to identify the underlying human need in the audience that might move them to action and if the audience is expected to be friendly, apathetic, unaware, or even hostile to the ideas you are suggesting. Be specific, knowing you can always adapt to different audiences later.
- **Step 3: Create**. Craft your narrative and develop your story. Consider what you want your audience to remember and how you want them to feel when determining your approach. Also consider how you will share your story. With a variety of mediums available in the workplace—ranging from conversational, to video call, to in person, to email—choose the path best for your specific story and desired outcome.

- **Step 4: Rehearse**. While it's true that practice makes perfect, the goal is to find the balance in being comfortable with the material while not memorizing a script. Tell your story to others that are not familiar with the topic and get their input.
- **Step 5: Inspire**. Deliver your story to the intended audience. Make note of their reaction, questions asked, and if the desired outcome was achieved. Was the level of detail appropriate? Do you need to continue telling the story to a different audience?
- **Step 6: Reflect**. Consider what you're trying to unlock with your story and what you want people to do. Were you successful? What adjustments may be needed for the next round?

Humanizing Data Insights Through Storytelling

Studies show that people retain only 5% to 10% of information that consists of statistics alone, but when they hear a story, they remember 65% to 70%.[4] This is one reason why data, or analytical, storytelling has become so important to the success of insights programs, including CX teams and has emerged as a critical job skill for these roles. At its core, data storytelling seeks to combine the data facts with a narrative, and often a visual to craft a more easily understood, relatable and memorable presentation for the audience.

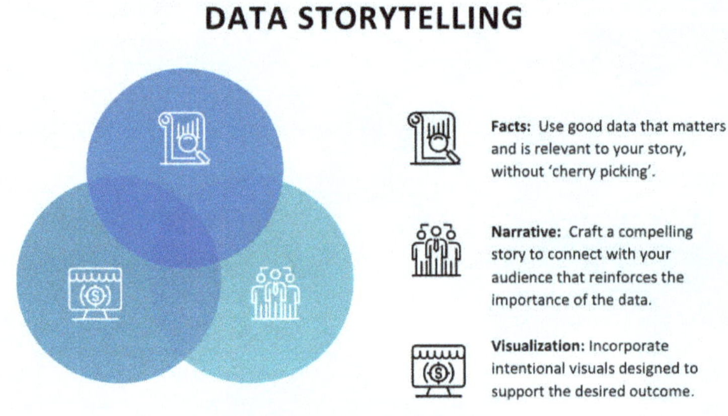

For CX Leaders, a common application is to create customer segment personas to highlight data and make the segments more relatable. These segments can then be widely leveraged across the enterprise—from journey mapping to agile development user stories to delivering personalized, tailored servicing support. Using this approach allows us to blend data with emotional storytelling to balance factual data with stories to gain a deeper understanding, make an impression or become more persuasive than by using the data alone.

However, despite a clear need for data storytelling, this can be a difficult skill to master. As suggested by Deloitte's Executive Perspectives article, many analysts may not be as comfortable crafting stories as others or may not feel they have the creative energy required to do so.[5] CX leaders may find the need to actively coach their insights team to ensure the 'so what' is clearly articulated in their messaging.

---

4   https://sarahklongerbo.com/blog/storytelling-in-marketing/

5   https://deloitte.wsj.com/cio/why-data-storytelling-is-so-important-and-why-were-so-bad-at-it-01671171516

Case Study #2: Using analytical storytelling to demonstrate a connection between CX impacts and strategic priorities.

A frequent reality is that CX leadership is all about influencing others, as it's exceedingly rare that a CX Leader fully owns an outcome single handedly and needs the support of others across the organization to mobilize change. During a recent online seminar discussing steps to secure executive investment to grow your CX program, I spoke about using analytical storytelling—using the data to create emotional connections with your stakeholders—as a technique to secure sponsorship and buying for your ideas.

In the online seminar, I asked attendees to imagine their brand just launched a new product, which has created significant demand and has potential to grow market share. It's an exciting time. Marketing is running a promo that is creating increased volume and sales. The company is betting big on this new product—it's the core of the strategic plan.

But your customers have questions and can't find all the answers online easily. The result is an increased call volume into customer care, resulting in extremely long wait times to speak to an agent. As the Call Center CX Leader, you have done all the analysis to know the impact of this poor customer experience and can see the impact across a range of metrics, including average speed of answer (ASA), abandonment rate, and overall ability to serve.

Historically, when call center operational issues spike, leadership defines the call center challenges and all the problems associated with the increased volume and articulates all the numbers and trends through a PowerPoint deck. But, this time, you, as the Call Center CX leader, take a different approach and instead reach out to the Product team to create a partnership. Together, you can illustrate how the contact center experience puts the new product launch at risk, which, in turn, has a clear tie to strategic priorities.

Together you craft an omnichannel narrative about the customer/product lifecycle that includes data-driven insights and 'what-if' business case analysis about the potential risks to the product launch if the customer experience call center issue was not resolved. The story was specifically created to capture executive attention, and it worked. As a result, the call center received the much needed up-stream support to address issues that were driving volume up, and the product team gained additional visibility into customer behaviors driven from the product launch. That was a Win-Win.

Spotlight on Understanding Your Audience

As we have reinforced throughout the chapter, the importance of understanding your audience and having a clear purpose in mind when crafting your narrative can not be underestimated. Know your audience. It's critical to take the time to understand your audience, including their unique needs, interests and personality, and tailor your story accordingly.

Take for example, Case Study #1: Inspiring Action through Experiential Storytelling. The CX leader here knew the Chief Operating Officer well enough to be confident he was a fun-loving soul that had deep empathy for the customer and genuinely wanted to understand their experience. The CX leader was certain the other executives would follow the COO's lead and not be offended or otherwise put off at being put in a position where they were brought face-to-face with the customers' challenges that the CX team was struggling to get resolved. With another personality type, it's easy to see how this same experiential storytelling approach may have had a vastly different outcome.

Take the time to analyze how you, as the CX Leader, can help your audience best reach their goals, or solve a particular business issue they are facing. If you are unsure about your audience's goals, do your due-diligence research and discovery, using the key question guide below, to ask around, talk to coworkers, or conduct informational interviews.

Tips and Techniques to Improve Storytelling Skills

While storytelling is an important tool in the CX Leader's tool kit, it may not always come naturally and may require some practice to find your unique approach. Here are some do's and don'ts to consider when crafting your narrative and practicing your presentation:

- Do make sure you are clear on your purpose and desired outcome. Consider a direct approach to your ask, if needed.
- Do make sure you test-drive your story. Try the 'coffee bar' test to see if you can tell your story over a cup of coffee with a friend or coworker.
- Do remember that storytelling should be fluid. It's ok to adjust your approach and modify the story based on each specific audience.
- Do consider different mediums and delivery techniques to increase engagement. For example, is there a relevant customer testimonial on social media? Consider embedding the video and then extending the story with data.
- Don't be overly worried about being too complete and including every detail and data point; instead, focus on the clarity of your message.
- Don't be too theoretical—CX practitioners can tend to be idealistic with their concepts, so be sure to include real-world and practical elements.
- Don't be afraid to adapt and change your story. Adjusting the details for each audience will help you tailor your narrative to the specific needs of each group.
- Don't take a one size fits all approach. If you deliver your story to different audiences, your idea may have numerous offshoots and variations within ONE central story.

Additionally, leverage resources such as watching TED Talks or attending local Toastmasters groups to practice public speaking and storytelling. TED Talks videos are a great way to observe a variety of storytelling techniques in a relatively short amount of time. Meanwhile, Toastmasters gives an opportunity to practice your storytelling skills in a safe environment, allowing you to work on skills such as leverage emotions in storytelling.

Reflection and Conclusion

CX leaders frequently find themselves needing to influence others and drive behavioral change. Learning to create and deliver successful CX stories can help secure investment and the resources necessary to execute CX strategy, resolve pain points, and inspire a customer-centric culture. The approach can bring an individual customer's journey to life in a way that reading a customer comment or seeing a survey score on a report cannot. When done well, a CX leader can use storytelling to intentionally invoke specific emotions like fear, anger, sentimentality, nostalgia, and doubt—all of which can be powerful motivators to influencing change and decision-making.

Recommended Reading:

1. The Persuasion Story Code: The Magic of Conversational Storytelling
2. Storytelling with Data: A Data Visualization Guide for Business Professionals
3. Everyday Business Storytelling: Create, Simplify, and Adapt a Visual Narrative for Any Audience
4. Unleash the Power of Storytelling: Win Hearts, Change Minds, Get Results

Chapter 8—The Emerging Role and Importance of AI in Managing the Customer Experience

Marc Mandel, CCXP

> *"AI is a tool. The choice about how it gets deployed is ours."*
> **Oren Etzioni, Professor Emeritus, University of Washington**

AI isn't new—it's just far more accessible.

There are few things more present in our conversational zeitgeist these days than AI and its impact on our personal and business lives, let alone, on society. Some argue that recent developments and breakthroughs in space have been excitingly revolutionary and others categorize them as fearful or even terrifying. Still, all would agree that AI arrived for many of us sometime over the past year and has irrevocably taken over the popular talk track. It's almost impossible to open a magazine or browse the web and not encounter significant editorial coverage about it, whether in its current form or speculatively, about the future ahead.

AI is not new and has been widely discussed and delivered for decades, both in academic and commercial circles. The year 2023 marked the beginning of what we'll call, "practical AI", where the once esoteric uses limited to large-scale corporate, military, or research purposes have become widely democratized and made available to you and me, often freely and in ways that even non-sophisticated users can appreciate and find benefit from.

How many of you can recall the first time you tried an early version of Netscape or even AOL's first internet browser 30+ years ago and first experienced the magic of the web? The Internet was not new, even back then, but it was the early browsers that emerged in the mid-1990s that made it readily available to mortals. Or, more recently, how many remember seeing the iPhone for the first time and dared to dream of carrying a phone and a full pocket computer with you that could serve as a true, digital assistant? Again, mobile phones existed long before the iPhone, but it was how the iPhone made pocket computing and mobile internet access truly available to the masses that allowed it to stand out and excite. In many ways, we are again at a Netscape or iPhone moment, but I will only see the adoption and impact explode for AI and how AI has been made available to you. This may prove, in time, to be as big or even bigger than the web or mobile, but that speculation will be for another time.

For the sake of argument, it may be prudent to describe here, for a moment, just what's meant by the term "Artificial Intelligence," or AI as it's easy to imagine that it can take on a variety of meanings depending on who's asked. For some, it's software to enable predictions of events that haven't happened quite yet, such as investment portfolio rebalancing based on future stock movements. For others, it could be an amazing content creation tool able to spit out a thoughtful blog article at the click of a mouse. For others still, it could replace an army of frontline service representatives in a company call center, fielding calls, chats, and emails and responding conversationally, in kind. For others, it could be a way to perform a detailed analysis of customer data ranging from survey responses to phone call recordings and CRM tickets to identify hard-to-spot trends and potentially customers who have unmet needs for either upselling or servicing.

For purposes of this commentary, let's agree to limit our consideration to just customer experience-related use cases, primarily these two; Analyzing customer feedback and transactional data and making service or sale recommendations by intelligently summarizing the results and modeling outcomes and the notion that AI can potentially replace a front line service representative and enable infinite engagement scale without the challenge of recruiting, managing, training and supporting a team of folks to do this work and the pitfalls that come with it.

From Eliza to GenAI: Evolution and Challenges in Chatbot Technology

First, a little history. Some of the earliest AI work that was made widely available to consumers looking to play and have fun dates to the mid-1970s with the personal computer application, "Eliza". Eliza was incredibly early, fun software that behaved like what we'd consider a chatbot-style interface—ask a simple question of Eliza, get a simple answer. "She" was set up to mimic a conversation with a psychotherapist and speak with you, with leading, open questions about yourself or your situation to which she'd share a quirky answer and then perhaps follow it with another leading question to keep the dialog rolling.

Here's an example of a conversation with Eliza.

User: I am feeling a bit sad today.

Eliza: I am sorry to hear you are sad.

User: Yes, it's because I had a fight with my friend.

Eliza: Tell me more about this fight with your friend.

User: Well, we disagreed over something trivial, and it just blew out of proportion.

Eliza: Why do you think the disagreement was blown out of proportion?

User: We were both stressed out over other things.

Eliza: What other things are you and your friend stressed about?

User: Work has been hectic for both of us, and it's taking a toll.

Eliza: How long has work been hectic?

User: For the past few months now.

Eliza: That must be hard. How have you been managing it?

User: Just trying to keep my head above water, really.

Eliza: You say you are just trying to keep your head above water. Can you elaborate on that?

No matter how conversationally compelling Eliza may seem, especially for its time, under the hood, it was little more than a bunch of rules crafted around specific keywords and phrases that could be easily spotted. Responses were hardwired into those same rules with a little wiggle room for variably placed phrases from the user's input to personalize the response. Remember, Eliza was nothing more than entertainment, but it also paved the way for more sophisticated use cases to follow.

Over the years, many companies were launched, touting to be the first, smart chatbot and outperforming the simplistic Eliza, even if built on remarkably similar rules (keyword and phrase spotting) logic. One such

company emerged in the late 1990s that originally started in Europe and later migrated to the US touting the use of intelligent chatbot technology delivered via website and used to direct users to specific parts of the site based on natural language (full sentence) input. Imagine, for example, asking the McDonald's website for nutritional information about their food offerings and being immediately directed to the right part of the site and the information would be easy to find. Now, further imagine the chatbot to have a little avatar, or animated character on the site to function as the face of the bot—think of Ronald McDonald, for example as the face of the chatbot for that McDonald's example or using a character like Clippy from the old Microsoft examples.

While built on a far more comprehensive vocabulary than the old Eliza, fundamentally the same logic was used in these tools, too. Keywords and hardwired phrases would be set up in the tool to "teach it" what to look for and how to phrase a response. The totality of these tools had to be preconceived in case the rule set of the software would fail to respond and ideally deflect the question rather than answer it incorrectly. Any overlooked input could create an erratic or completely incorrect response or misdirect the conversation flow into unplanned and incorrect ways. Even with the increase in sophistication, these companies all failed to capture a market and eventually went out of business. These early tools, much like the Eliza example were not forgotten, however, and in many ways, laid important groundwork for the advancements we are seeing today.

Broadly, the promise of AI and specifically, generative AI (GenAI) is built on these early technology ancestors with the most notable leaving the hard-coded keywords and phrases behind in the past and more modern machine learning techniques used to begin to truly train the machine to find patterns in the user input and then identify meaning in the patterns found. An innate ability emerged to teach the computer to, in effect, learn from those patterns and become able to link them back to responses or other data and surface information immediately against an almost endless set of conversational use cases. It's easy to imagine a time when a huge army of call center agents could diminish or even be eliminated and replaced by smart AI agents ready to serve customers regardless of their conversational needs. The potential to save countless millions of dollars that typically get invested in these frontline teams—from hiring to termination—could be reduced to zero and could prove to be the holy grail for many. Except, no, not yet. Even today, in 2024, with all the advancements we've seen, it's clear that this technology is not prime-time ready and in fact, presents new liability risks and other challenges to early adopters.

AI in Customer-Facing Applications Needs Governance

There was a 2024 news story about just such a case. Air Canada, the great Canadian national airline, deployed GenAI chatbot technology in its frontline service center and exposed it to customers, to mitigate further support cost increases while still maintaining reasonable service levels. The chatbot was configured and made available to travelers contacting Air Canada looking for customer service, to update travel arrangements or cancel previously booked itineraries. In one customer interaction the customer inquired via the chatbot about refund policies and the AI bot responded in-kind and indeed offered the customer a refund when in fact, that decision went against policy and was subsequently denied. The customer was outraged and made a case out of the prior promise of a refund, even though in this case, the refund was inappropriately offered and they prevailed, and Air Canada was forced to comply and provide refunds to many customers they would have otherwise avoided. While this cautionary tale of an AI-infused chatbot seems like a minor mishap and only cost the company the price of a single airfare, imagine for a moment if it wasn't Air Canada but rather a large pharmaceutical company equivalently engaging their customers, dispensing sensitive health information and recommendations instead of a human expert, counterpart.

The risks that the AI engine might "make up an answer" are both very real and exceedingly high. Worse, at least in current terms, it's difficult to discern fact from what AI researchers have termed, "hallucinations" where the machine simply invents a compelling-sounding response but is not in any way adherent to policy or fact. That pharmaceutical company in the hypothetical example could see itself in profoundly serious trouble if an AI chatbot made healthcare commendations that resulted in illness or worse. The liability would be unprecedented and off-the-chart.

The moral of this story is simple. No matter how exciting the idea of being able to replace many customer-facing service representatives with an AI system is, it's not for the faint of heart at this time and should not be entered lightly. The likelihood that these machines will make errors, and sometimes significant ones with major implications, is very real and the risks associated are significant in most cases.

Redirect AI from customer-facing to employee-enabling!

An exception could be a basic frontline engagement model that could replace what is traditionally managed by a "dumb" IVR system for call direction and routing and could be dramatically improved from a customer experience standpoint with an AI-based bot. The bot could be trained to execute a lifelike conversation regardless of voice, email, chat, SMS, or whatever other modality was needed and just be used as a first customer touchpoint to capture information and do some simplistic triage before routing the request up the chain to a person to step in and oversee it. This AI-based first touch could make an arcane process of "dial 1 for sales, 2 for service", etc., and the irritating call tree that tends to follow into more of a lifelike conversation and then simple redirection the moment enough information has been gathered and understood. This "tier 1" use-case mindset has very real and very practical value and presents little if any material risk to either the company or the customer.

While these examples may at first appear dated or over-simplistic, the reality is that while on one hand, they are indeed so, they do still reflect the state of the technology circa 2024 relative to customer-facing, conversational, bot-enabled use cases. In effect, they force us to pose a very delicate balance between a limited vocabulary delivered by very rigid linguistic rules and simple Boolean if-then statements, and the risk of generating unanticipated results that could bring about new risks and liabilities if machine-generated responses in effect, go off the reservation and respond in unanticipated and unacceptable ways.

We will begin to see these problems lift as we look into the near future and it's highly likely that from mid-2025 and beyond, we'll see much more control and governance brought to this technology. The likelihood of rogue responses based on made-up logic will become increasingly unlikely. The utilization of private language models tailored to individual organizations and customer language patterns will augment their value and impact on customer experience, reliability, and trustworthiness.

Real World CX Use Case #1: Agent Assist

For the present and near future, a more effective application of AI tools in CX lies in their utilization for internal purposes rather than customer-facing interactions. These tools are best employed to enhance employee efficiency and effectiveness in serving customers. By integrating a knowledgeable intermediary between the AI and the customer, acting as an intelligent filter, these tools can significantly benefit both employees and customers alike.

The research organization, Gartner Group, originated the use of the term AI more so as "augmented intelligence" than the more typical artificial intelligence vernacular. That said, the Gartner description may be more appropriate as the technology can function as a rocket fuel of sorts in how it can increase individual productivity, efficiency, and overall effectiveness.

Imagine a use-case in that same frontline customer contact center, but now, instead of deploying AI tools instead of agents, it is deployed to the agent and accessible as part of the representative's desktop environment. The AI can be set up to automatically listen to a call or monitor a chat stream and in effect, pop-up messages on the agent's screen with recommendations of how best to manage almost any typical situation that may arise in customer interactions. The AI can be set up to be a silent coach to representatives, unobtrusively prompting them with suggestions about policy and solutions to problems without the more typical need for the agent to continually ask the customer for patience while they search for answers in knowledge bases and help wikis. Agent effort would decrease dramatically as would typically call-handling times while a high likelihood of improved first-contact resolution and increased overall customer satisfaction.

Call center leaders are struggling to maintain adequate staffing levels these days, with an average head-count turnover in midsize contact centers of more than 50% per year and with some centers reporting turn-over at more than 100% annually. The cost to replace a burned-out agent could in many cases within the US approach $40,000 or more per headcount replacement between lost productivity, replacement sourcing, training, and onboarding a replacement and the replacement having to learn on their own and through tribal knowledge to become conversant quickly enough to be effective.

Inward-facing AI applications offer invaluable support to agents by alleviating fatigue and mitigating the risk of burnout, streamlining administrative tasks associated with handling customer inquiries, and significantly reducing post-call activities such as disposition and note-taking, all of which can eat into productivity. These tools can be trained using typical customer queries and deployed in a supervised manner, exclusively accessible to staff and not directly exposed to customers—at least for the time being—thus ensuring their efficacy in this controlled environment.

How often have you dialed a customer service line only to be placed on hold while the representative searches through lengthy help files for an answer? With AI, this process is revolutionized. Instead of tedious searches, the software swiftly retrieves specific information snippets in real time, providing representatives with AI-generated recommendations and offers for the next best action. Additionally, by analyzing tone, including inflection and speech rate, AI can detect customer emotions. If elevated, the system can assist agents in deflection strategies, enhancing the overall customer experience. Deploying these tools in such a manner harnesses their considerable capabilities while minimizing risks, making AI integration not only sensible but also remarkably negligible risk.

Real World CX Use Case #2: Serving the Analyst

A related but slightly different use case for AI is to consider its use as a helpful part of a typical data analyst's work. The CX profession is chock full of analysts eager to sink their claws into the latest dataset from the VoC, call center, or marketing automation platforms and to slice and dice it for insight. We know that it's not an easy task and one that can often be very time-consuming and labor-intensive. Interestingly, these same insights often have a shockingly short shelf life and the longer the analyst spends consuming and generating meaningful insights from the data, the less valuable those results tend to be. Speed, it seems, is of the essence, but speed without accuracy is a recipe for disaster.

What if it was possible to feed your recent VoC results as a raw data file into a simple AI tool and simply prompt it with questions like, "What are the top 3 things this data is telling us?" or, "Which topics in this file are most negative or most positive, and why?" or even, "What are the biggest sources of negative feedback and what interventions can be done to alleviate them?" and be able to get at least directional results in seconds, almost regardless of the amount of feedback presented? How incredible would it be for that same analyst who might have taken three days to crunch the data to now get at least top-line insights at the push of a button and then redirect their valuable time to strategy and key formulaic recommendations?

It's easy to see a use case for AI to help us navigate increasingly complex data sets that are typical in CX as the number of measured interactions continues to increase. AI, in this capacity, could create world-class superhumans from average analysts. To those ends, while there's been considerable industry chatter that AI tools pose a risk of outright replacing researchers and analysts, the more likely outcome is that they will do just the opposite and add tremendous value by augmenting the analysts' ability and speed and make them that much more valuable.

A variety of AI-infused analytical tools hit the market in recent months, some more powerful than others, but all of them have positive implications and potential impact on augmenting the analyst's abilities to find those increasingly elusive nuggets of insight in CX data. For example, it's easy enough to use a $20 per month ChatGPT subscription and drop a spreadsheet file of survey results into it and ask for insights. ChatGPT will be happy to fill your screen with key findings and depending on how prompted, corresponding recommendations. The need for high-end specialized tools that could cost many thousands of dollars seems to be limited and that need is steadily decreasing by the day in place of far less expensive, primarily open-source options. It would not take an expert to imagine a future where it's easy enough to link a low-priced or free tool like ChatGPT for example to a data reporting and visualization tool like Tableau or Power BI and, in that combination, provide the large-scale enterprise software options a real run for their money. That future is, remarkably, just around the corner.

Regardless of whether you're part of a front-line service center organization or regularly perform customer data analytics as your primary role at work, it could be easy to fall prey to fearmongering about how the emergent recent technology will displace you and lose your job to it. This, however, at least for now, could not be farther from the truth. The risk of AI doing your job for you, and more to the point, without you, is not sound thinking for now in 2024 as this is being written and the latest innovations are rolling out. The models and delivery technology are just not ready enough, or frankly, "human enough" to do that. Augmenting the professional, however, is a very real and advantageous use case in either front-line or analytical roles which should not make us fearful but instead excited.

Imagine, for example, knowing what we know now if we were afraid that early desktop computers were about to cause office workers to lose their jobs when they first showed up on the scene in the early 1980s, replacing typewriters. Sure, typewriters lost their jobs, but we did not. Or imagine when the Internet became more available in the mid-1990s with the beginnings of the accessible worldwide web if we lost our jobs? No, that didn't happen. We all went online and became orders of magnitude more productive. The same thing happened with the early adoption of smartphones in the early 2000s. Productivity skyrocketed but we were not at risk. AI, if considered in this way, will be the same thing, playing out again now with our productive output again being pushed to new heights but there is negligible risk or downside to those who learn to harness its power.

The near-term win for companies and employees with AI all lies in that productivity multiplier effect. In the early days of personal computing, Steve Jobs of Apple famously quoted research done by <u>Scientific American</u> magazine when they studied what made certain animals able to move more quickly than others while at the same time, requiring less expenditure of energy to achieve high speeds. Jobs referred to the large bird, the Condor, as being the most productive locomotive, able to soar faster than other animals while expending the least energy to do that. Sadly, man, he said, was far down the list. Interestingly, Jobs, self-serving then added that giving a man a bicycle to maximize his locomotion propelled him to the top of the list, besting even the majestic condor. He was, at the time, comparing the effect the bicycle had on propulsion to the impact computers have on office workers and how computers uniquely helped even average producers become super-producers.

The Future of AI in CX

It shouldn't take a powerful crystal ball to imagine the future of AI and the impact it will have on customer engagement and experience. With a truly unprecedented amount of investment being made into the companies behind it, we'll likely see amazing advancements made overnight. OpenAI, the company behind the amazing ChatGPT, for example, is hard at work refining their next-generation models that will power future versions of their software that if successful, could render it indiscernible from human intelligence. One of the holy grails in AI research work is referred to as "AGI," or, Artificial General Intelligence which will make ChatGPT able to understand everything in the total of human knowledge, give or take a little bit. They say things are "on track" to release this sometime in 2025 or 2026 and assuming they do, there will be almost no limit to its potential.

It's a genuinely exciting time to see these developments and those that have recently led to them and the impact this work will have on not only customer experience but on humanity. Until then, the story is more of an optimistic, yet cautionary tale and one that should not dissuade you from creative experimentation with AI in how you serve your customers and empower the frontline. The immediate potential is nothing short of amazing if used in responsible and governed ways and is still further evolving. Don't blink or you might just miss its grand arrival.

Chapter 9—The CX Professional as a Trusted Guide

Mark Slatin

> *"The more clients trust you, the more they will bring you in on more advanced, complex, strategic issues."*
>
> **Charles H. Green, Co-author, *The Trusted Advisor***

The Executive Boardroom—Setting the Stage

Steve's anxiety grew as he pushed the button for the 10th floor on the elevator. He climbed ever closer to the Millard R. Wayneright Executive Boardroom, renowned for its ostentatious decor reminiscent of a bygone era. The fox hunting artwork and the green winged back chairs greeted him in the room known facetiously as the "on deck circle." His pulse quickened. Sweat began to bead on his palms as he battled his inner critic, acutely aware of the high stakes involved. Finally, the handle turned from the inside of the mahogany door and a voice called his name, "Steve…you ready?"

His heart raced as he entered the boardroom. The portraits of all the Bank's former presidents completed the museum-like aura of the space. Smiling was not exceedingly popular back then. Like a matador entering the bullring, Steve knew the outcome of this encounter could shape the trajectory of CX initiatives within this financial institution. Considering the gravity of the situation, it begged the question: What could have alleviated Steve's heightened anxiety before stepping into the boardroom?

The Crossroads of CX Leadership

Long before Steve's encounter with the C-Suite, the seeds of success or failure were sown. The narrative of CX disciplines often oscillates between triumph and stagnation, with many initiatives faltering on the path to achieving sustainable results. In the world of customer experience management (CXM), the journey to success often leads through the high-stakes terrain of the C-Suite. This chapter explores the unique challenges, sobering realities, and common mistakes that CX leaders encounter. Then we'll also look at four keys that will empower them to unlock meaningful transformation.

The ROI of CX is Insufficient

Experts in the field often zero in on one critical factor: the failure to substantiate the return on investment (ROI) of CX initiatives. CX leaders find themselves in a perpetual struggle to justify the resources they seek from the executive echelon. While they compete for funding alongside other business units, presenting a mere spreadsheet with ROI projections will fall short of convincing the decision-makers.

That's because contrary to common belief, members of the executive team are not impervious to the sway of emotions. Even C-suite executives, often perceived as entirely bottom-line focused, are influenced by their emotions. According to Harvard Professor Gerald Zaltman, a staggering 95% of thought, emotion, and learning occur in the recesses of the unconscious—a realm devoid of conscious awareness. Decisions are driven by emotion and subsequently rationalized with logic.

Consequently, relying on what appears to be a rock-solid business case can get derailed if you aren't perceived as trustworthy. And it's not limited to the executive team; CX leaders must build trusted relationships at all levels of their organization. This imperative is non-negotiable because CX practitioners grapple with the cold, hard realities of operating within constraints such as small teams, minuscule budgets, and limited positional authority. In navigating these challenges, they must get things done by leveraging their ability to influence others. That makes trust non-negotiable. How can you become a trusted guide who serves as a catalyst to embed CX into their company's culture?

The ***TRUSTED GUIDE ROADMAP™ Master Class*** is built on four essential principles, as illustrated below, that I wish I had known during my time as a CX practitioner.

The Four Keys—The Foundation of CX Leadership

1. **Earning Trust**—trust underpins a CX leader's ability to lead change.
2. **Becoming a Guide**—stakeholders are not seeking another hero, but they might just be open to a guide.
3. **Building a CX Roadmap**—a strategic plan that keeps the mission on track and engages the C-Suite.
4. **Proving the Value**—explains how the investment will produce a return (not just in dollars and sense).

Let's dive deeper into each of these essential components that underpin effective CX leadership.

1. Earning Trust

Trust forms the bedrock of any successful CX initiative. Charles H. Green, renowned author of *The Trusted Advisor*, offers a succinct formula known as *The Trust Equation*.

This equation comprises four key variables:

- **Credibility:** Offering accuracy of information shared, coupled with confidence and candor (not arrogance).
- **Reliability:** Demonstrating predictability and follow-through, displaying active listening.

- **Intimacy:** Fostering psychological safety for vulnerability and sensitive conversations.
- **Self-Orientation:** Ensuring an "other" orientation, devoid of self-serving interests.

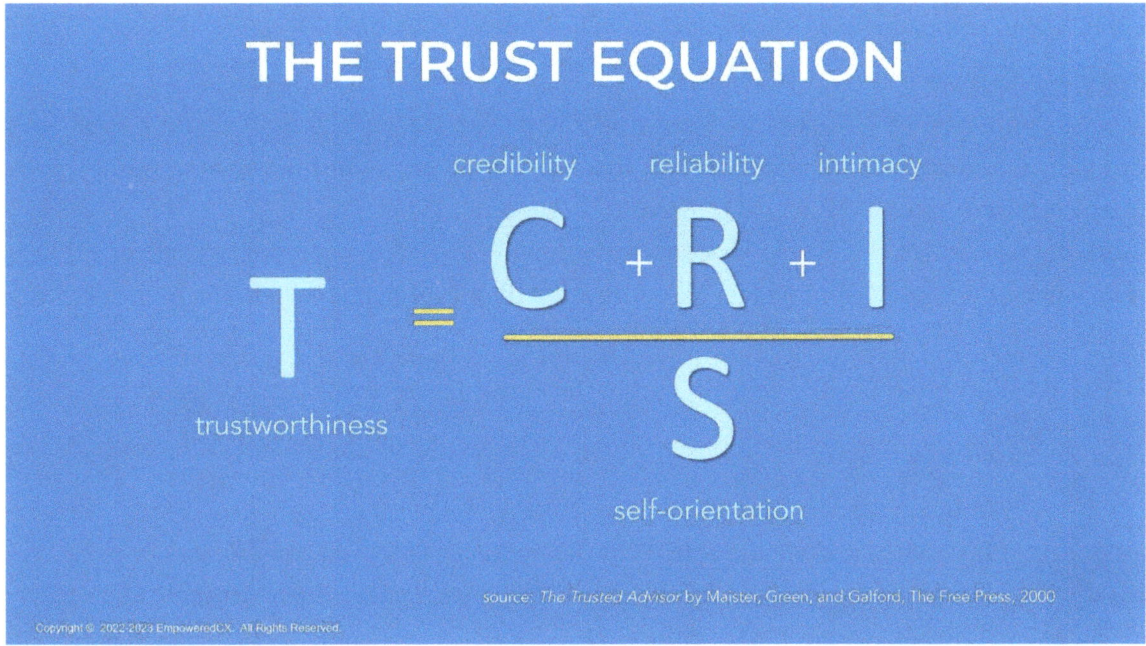

Here's an overview of the variables and some practical tips on how to improve in each one:

Credibility—Double check all your data for clarity and accuracy. You don't want to erode trust by confusing your audience (or be perceived as the hero which we'll talk about in the next section). Lastly, credibility has to do with the words you choose. Speak in their language and speak confidently.

Reliability—Follow through on what you say you'll do. This centers on predictability; the use of a CX Roadmap (which we'll dive into later), consistent metrics, and a CX dashboard will help with this component.

Intimacy—an odd word in a business context but *The Trusted Advisor* authors used it intentionally. Intimacy has to do with psychological safety. Here are a few tips on how to increase trustworthiness through intimacy: be fully present and take notes on what they share. Listen empathetically; validate their thoughts and feelings. Keep confidential information private.

Self-orientation—this is in the denominator of the equation because it has an inverse relationship to trustworthiness. This variable is a matter of focus…whether others perceive you are focused on you or on them. For CX leaders, it extends beyond focusing on **your** own outcomes and pushing **your** agenda and includes subtleties such as a preoccupation with a past or future event. Get grounded and be fully present.

To succeed regarding the four trust variables, one must be aware of personal tendencies and actively improve them. Low trust levels jeopardize the acceptance of even the most compelling ROI models, often leading to unspoken barriers hindering progress. Trust serves as the linchpin for catalyzing meaningful change.

For more on how CX leaders can apply the four trust variables, listen to my interview with *Trusted Advisor* co-author Charles H. Green: *Building Trust with Key Stakeholders* on The *Delighted Customers Podcast*. [www.empoweredcx.com/podcast]

2. Becoming a Guide

In the dynamic landscape of CX, success hinges on the perception of CX leaders not merely as agents of change, but indispensable guides. Donald Miller's *Building a Story Brand* outlines four archetypal roles present in every narrative: hero, guide, victim, and villain.

The **hero** of the story is a character who wants something but needs to overcome a challenge. The **guide** has been the hero many times and can provide wisdom through their experience to help the hero achieve their goal.

Warning: striving to be the hero is ill-fated.
The reason is simple:

Your key stakeholders don't want another hero!
It's easy to assume the role of the subject matter expert, tossing out
CX jargon while positioning yourself as the smartest person in the room.
That's playing the hero role.
Yes, it's tempting to fall into that trap.
But it's stealing the hero's thunder.

And if you swoop in to play the role of the hero, they will:

- Withdraw
- Shutdown
- Stonewall
- Ghost

What's worse, they won't tell you that's what they're doing.

I'll never forget the time when I tried to push through an initiative for a CX metric's adoption as a bank-wide metric. I made the mistake of not getting the full support of one of the business unit leaders who felt threatened by the metric. In my impatience and excitement to make progress, I alienated a key stakeholder and caused the initiative to go sideways- for three years. Ouch!

Instead of stepping into the hero role and inadvertently stealing their thunder, be their guide!

The guide cares more about helping the stakeholder to achieve their goals and aspirations than their own. And the stakeholder sees the guide as a genuine aid to help them win.

Consider these hero/guide partners:
- Dorothy/Glinda, the good witch (*Wizard of Oz*)
- Daniel/Mr. Miyagi (*Karate Kid*)
- Luke Skywalker/Yoda (*Star Wars*)

The key to serving as a guide is to deeply understand and build trust with your stakeholders.

Stakeholders crave guidance, not heroics, and steering them towards success demands empathy, humility, and a relentless focus on their aspirations. By embracing the role of a trusted guide, CX leaders cultivate authentic relationships, foster collaboration, and drive sustained progress.

3. Building a Roadmap

Our friend Steve could enhance the confidence of the C-Suite and bolster his credibility by guiding the portfolio of CX projects with a CX Roadmap.

Why? With a meticulously crafted CX roadmap in hand, CX leaders can effectively pinpoint areas of improvement using established frameworks. By methodically charting this roadmap, businesses gain the foresight to anticipate and mitigate potential pain points before they escalate. More importantly, C-Suite leaders are constantly weighing organizational risk.

A customer experience roadmap that fosters collaboration among key stakeholders and is in harmony with corporate objectives reduces risk in the minds of executives while positioning the CX Leader as a guide rather than a hero.

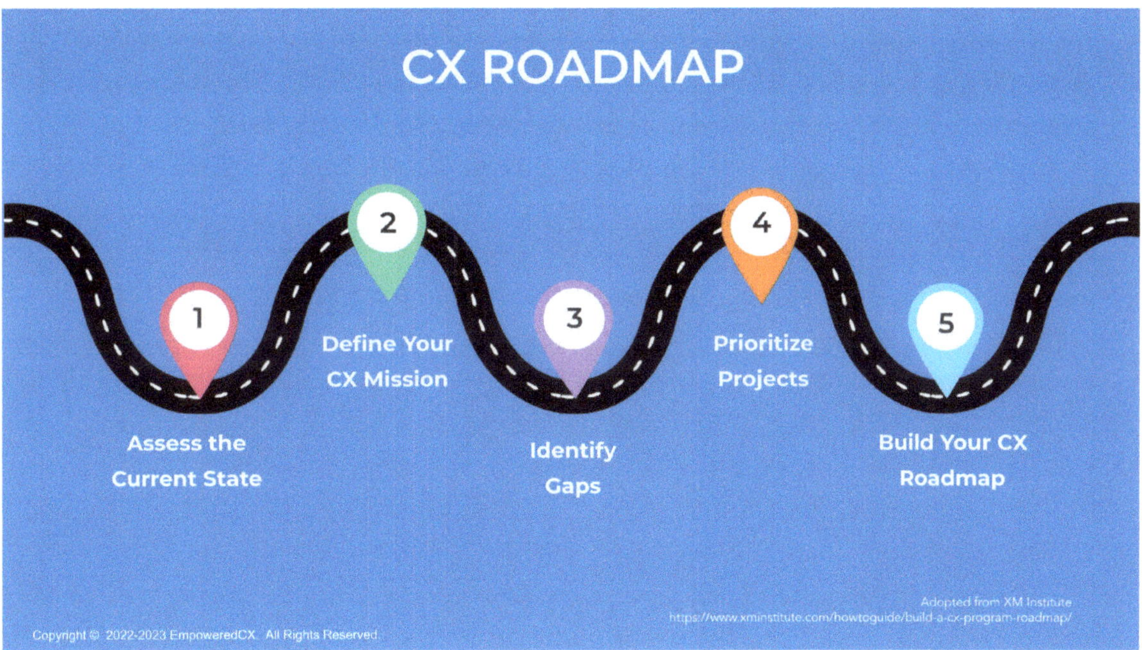

So, how does one construct a CX roadmap that guarantees successful transformation? Here's a concise five-step guide:

1. **Assess the Current State:** Begin by conducting an experience maturity assessment to gauge your organization's current standing. The assessment we use in the Master Class is organized by the five categories requisite for CCXP Certification. It provides valuable insights and serves as a baseline.

2. **Craft your CX Mission and Principles:** Clarify the decision-making processes and strategic frameworks governing CX initiatives. Think of this step as setting the GPS coordinates for your journey, guiding you towards your destination.

3. **Identify the Gaps:** Compile a comprehensive list outlining the disparities between your organization's current CX state and the desired future state. This exercise lays the groundwork for targeted improvement efforts.

- **Prioritize Projects:** Recognize that resources are finite, and not all initiatives can be pursued simultaneously. Utilize a prioritization framework to identify and allocate resources to projects that yield the greatest impact.

- **Build Your CX Roadmap:** Synthesize the insights gathered from the previous steps into a cohesive roadmap spanning two to three years. This blueprint serves as a strategic guide, steering your organization towards its CX objectives.

Much like a well-planned vacation promises relaxation and enjoyment, a thoughtfully constructed CX roadmap facilitates acceptance of recommendations, propels progress on CX projects, and will help to secure a seat at the decision-making table.

4. Proving Value

"The notion that executive decision-making is purely rational is a convenient fiction. It begins through the filter of logic but quickly shifts to emotion, the primary motivator. Finally, logic returns as rationalization to justify their emotions. That means, leaders who want to impact change need to connect first on an emotional level."

Charles H. Green, Co-author, *The Trusted Advisor*

While the merits of CX initiatives may be self-evident, articulating their value in financial terms is essential for garnering support from the C-Suite. Despite the inevitable influence of emotions, having something quantifiable will meet their requirement for justifying their decision. CX leaders should avoid using complicated CX metrics that executives might not understand. Instead, they should explain the results using words and concepts that relate to what the organization wants to achieve. Whether it's revenue growth, cost reduction, or enhanced profitability, demonstrating tangible business value is paramount. Moreover, aligning CX outcomes with organizational priorities fosters alignment and ensures CX initiatives receive the attention and resources they deserve.

For example, if this year's organizational goal is growing top line revenue, stating outcomes of CX efforts in these terms is much more likely to enlist C-level support. One of the most common potholes that CX leaders fall into (I know I did) is speaking the language of CX instead of speaking the language of the C-Suite. NPS, CSAT, Journey Mapping, VoC, is often just jargon in the ears of executives and positions you as an outsider.

Translate enablers such as NPS surveys, journey mapping, and experience design into measurable financial outcomes. Articulate the anticipated returns on investment (ROI) in terms of revenue expansion, expense mitigation, or enhanced profitability.

The following diagram illustrates the models we use in **The Trusted Guide Roadmap™** Master Class that includes templates and calculators in the "Prove the Value" Module.

5. ROI Models that "Prove the Value:"

1. **Statistical inference**—using macro data to infer related outcomes.
2. **Net Revenue Retention**—comparing the same customer set over a period as a percentage, accounting for revenue expansion and customer churn.
3. **Cost Efficiency**—calculating company cost savings resulting from a CX initiated change.
4. **Share of Wallet**—measuring the growth of customer spend as a percentage of their total spend potential.

Loyalty Driver Focus—identifying which customer touchpoints generate the most loyalty and calculating fiscal impact of experience changes.

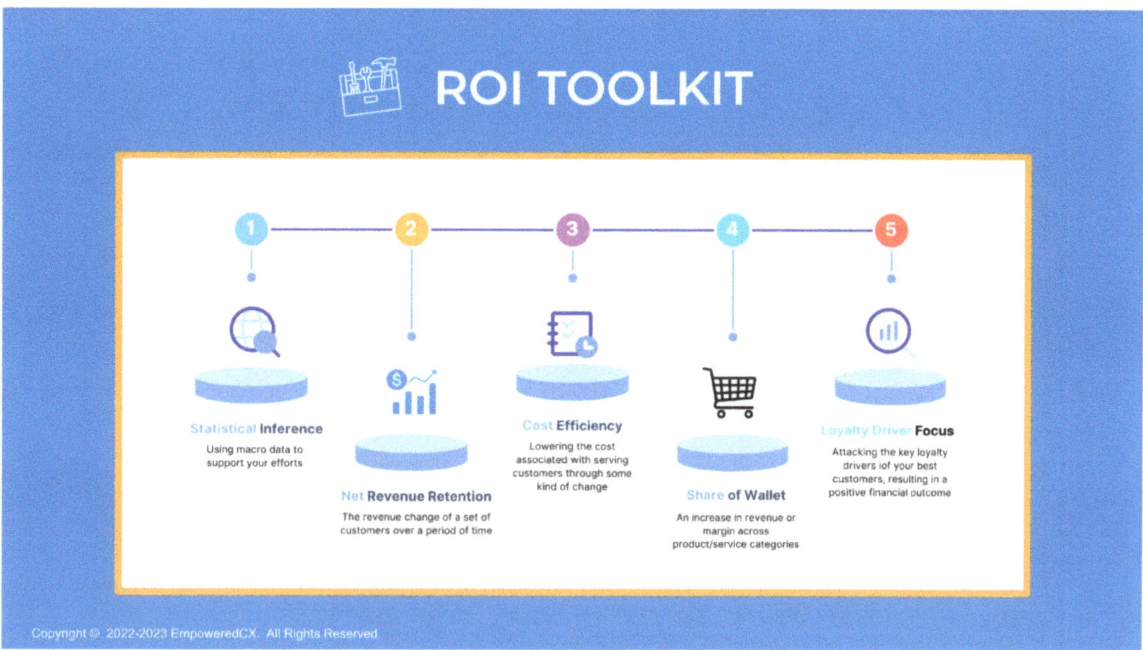

By no means is this list intended to be all-inclusive or even the best choice for your organization. In fact, each organization should develop ROI metrics unique to their needs. But it does provide a core set of models that CX leaders can iterate from.

As we've seen through Steve's experience, the outcomes of these encounters can shape the trajectory of CX initiatives within an organization. If you are a CX leader, I commend you for the important work that you're doing. I know it's not easy. But by embracing the four keys outlined in this chapter—earning trust, becoming guides, crafting strategic roadmaps, and proving the value—you will make a difference in the lives of your customers. These keys empower you to navigate challenges adeptly, foster authentic relationships, and drive sustained progress.

An Alternate Ending

Prior to being armed with these four keys, Steve felt like a matador going into a bullring. But now Steve can realize an alternative ending in a different arena.

In 1980, a miracle happened on ice. In one of the most unlikely David and Goliath stories in modern times, the US Olympic Hockey team defeated the Soviet Union team. The Americans, a hodge-podge of college players, were strangers from rival teams. They had to skate against a hand-selected band of All Star veterans. Their coach, Herb Brooks, earned their trust because he demonstrated his knowledge of hockey (credibility), prepared tirelessly (reliability), expressed his belief in everyone (intimacy), and put the emphasis on teamwork rather than individual performance (low self-orientation).

The victory over the Soviets didn't start the night of the game…it started months before as Brooks earned the trust of his players by becoming a trusted guide.

> *"Leadership is not taken, it is given. Leadership is given to those that they trust. They allow people they trust to have influence over their lives."*
>
> **Henry Cloud**

Chapter 10—Using CX to Act

Ken Peterson

"Confidence is what you gain after taking action, not before."

Felecia Etienne

A Love Story

This is not a Taylor Swift song, but I am reminded of a story from my past. There was a young man and a young woman who attended different high schools roughly three hours apart from each other. Through high school athletics, they had a chance to be introduced to each other through a mutual acquaintance. Immediately sparks flew, but being young and both lacking self-confidence, neither of them would take the first significant step. In a sense, they kept measuring the room every time they saw each other. Despite some opportune moments, no action was ever taken.

Those two would go on to live their own lives, have families of their own and careers of which many would be envious. However, it was not until a chance meeting many years later that they disclosed to each other and mutually discovered the once still intense feelings they had for each other. If one or the other had acted during that initial phase in their bonding, there may have been a completely different story to tell. Perhaps one more fitting of a Taylor Swift song.

Action is Everything

For me, one of the biggest takeaways is that no matter how much assessing, understanding and insight is gathered, if no action is taken, you are likely to lose out on a relationship. In personal relationships, it often is not the fault of any one person and the same can be true in a relationship the brand has with a customer. However, the impact of inaction within all the brand-to-consumer relationships is undoubtedly felt more by the brand than by the consumer.

The dance is pretty much the same. There is a courtship (Attention/Awareness), where the consumer's journey with the brand relationship begins. Then, suddenly eyes meet from across the room, the consumer has seen what is out there, determines they like what they see in the brand (Interest/Desire). Then, the consumer walks across the room and initiates a conversation (Desire/Purchase Decision) giving the brand the first hint that there is something of a connection between them. However, if that bond is not validated by the brand, it is likely that the relationship will not go any further (Action/Retention). While those were the four phases in the customer journey in the AIDA model, more recently we can also think about the fifth phase, and without that one, there will not likely be lifelong stories to tell about that brand-to-consumer relationship (Advocacy).

Sometimes actions are small, sometimes they are more significant. The magnitude of actions usually depends on a few factors—the size of a single transaction, potential lifetime value of the transactions, and the profitability of ongoing transactions.

CX Gone Wrong

When I first entered the field of Customer Experience it had a different name back then and many brands were adhering to the supply chain management system called the Service-Profit Chain looking to make the connections between employee satisfaction, customer loyalty, productivity, and profitability.

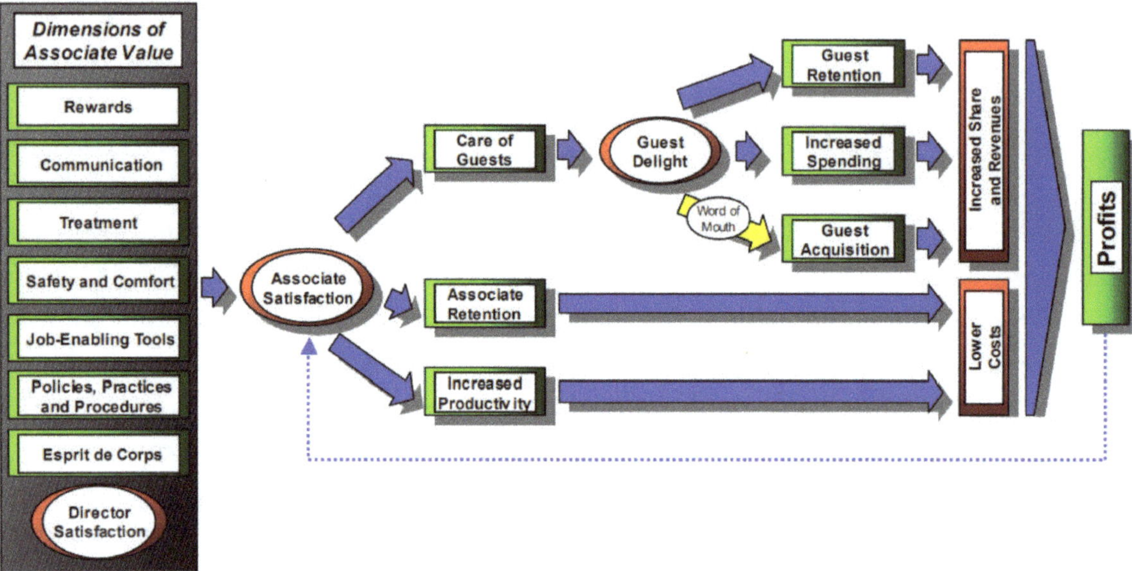

Back then, getting a few moments of the consumer's time represented an opportunity to have a conversation with them. Often, the feedback was gathered by a printed survey or a telephone call and an incentive was provided for them to act on the survey. Surveys tended to be longer and asked many questions about the details of the interaction or the relationship. That data often took time to get back to the frontlines as it was frequently gathered quarterly (though sometimes monthly), aggregated, and sent to the brand, and then after a review, it was sent to the frontline teams. While the insights could be dated, a key aspect of the research was that a user had insights that could be used to act—even if there was not a firm starting point for that action or clarity on the benefit of that action.

Then in 2003, a researcher Frederick F. Reichheld proposed the idea that only one question was truly needed to gauge the potential growth of a company. The idea really did not discredit the Service-Profit Chain model that had been frequently used to show the connection between loyalty and profitability, rather it attempted to demonstrate that the question of "Likelihood to Recommend" was the strongest predictive measurement related to the future growth of a company based on the idea that the relationship between the customer and the brand were strong.

With just a mere suggestion that one question can help predict the future of a company and the growing use of a trend, considered by some to be a "passing fad," called the internet, brands started to focus on that one question and the hope of a more complete sampling of the population through the cheaper medium of online surveys.

There were several problems with this approach:

1. The Net Promoter Score as proposed by Frederick Reichheld is essentially based on relationship with the customer (suited to a Customer Experience Relationship research study) but is often used incorrectly in Transactional Customer Experience surveys, a less-than-optimal approach even acknowledged by the author.
2. Due to the ease of conducting such studies and the draw of recency in gathering feedback, Transactional Customer Experience surveys dominate in the internet era and combined with the wide acceptance of Net Promoter Score, these go hand in hand.
3. While having a compelling connection to business growth, the Net Promoter Score has no practical insights coming from that one question, therefore it was proposed to add a single open-ended question.
4. The addition of the open-ended question was intended to yield insights into acting, but early thematic analysis was limited and often pushed to manual coding of comments (saying goodbye to any cost savings). NLP, Semantic Analytics and Generative AI took years to be even remotely reliable, and even now the reliability of the results is easily questionable.
5. Even without great reliability, the use of themes and semantic analysis was primarily used to get another score or build another chart instead of understanding the ability and worthiness of specific actions.
6. To overcome the limited amount of insights, more questions are being added to get more data to help drive insights. Lengthening the survey and reducing participation.
7. Each of those questions needed a way to be understood, so Customer Experience technology platforms focused on building more widgets, and less about the actions associated with the data being collected and analyzed.
8. Incentives were introduced to encourage individuals to improve their measurements. Customer Experience scores became vanity metrics for some organizations and a source of additional income for frontline managers.
9. With incentives, the focus shifted to moving the dial on the important Customer Experience scores. Instead of looking at an individual response as a learning opportunity, a negative score on feedback was questioned—sometimes to management and other times to the customer themselves—further decreasing the customer experience.
10. When scores were good, managers focused on the employee impact of those scores in a detrimental way—creating friction between frontline managers and their employees as well as impacting the relationship with customers—sometimes to the extent that gaming of the surveys took place.
11. As scores failed to move and participation decreased, varied teams within brands started fighting for control of the "big measurement program" because that meant budget and control of the measurements and incentives. This took programs away from the "action" teams such as Operations and Customer Care and folded them into Marketing.
12. Inevitably, when budgets must be tightened up, the program that "shows no movement" is quickly put on the chopping block—either cut or offered to the lowest bidder through a procurement process that has little interest in the current and future needs of such a program in an enterprise.
13. Finally, when looking to justify the spend for collecting data about Net Promoter Score, there arose a significant amount of research that placed into question the true ability to demonstrate potential future growth by simply asking the "ultimate question."

Each time a new problem is solved by the latest and greatest analytics trend, another setback in the approach is uncovered or the dynamics of the buyers shift so significantly as to limit the usefulness of the data and the insights gathered from these ever-shifting approaches. Despite all the analytical limitations that can happen, there is still a good reason to conduct Customer Experience research beyond gathering a score.

Actions That Fix The Problem

Many years ago, my role included working with software companies specializing in Customer Experience measurement and reporting. This gave me the opportunity to understand what each software featured and decide for my clients which tool provided the best opportunity to help our clients get what they wanted. Many elements of the offer were the same for all these providers: a focus on transactional surveys, based mostly on the Net Promoter Score and dashboards with many chart options.

A couple of these companies stood out to me for various reasons surrounding their closed-loop feedback options. Closed-loop feedback can be one of the most effective tools in a Customer Experience measurement platform. It is the process of acting on feedback—often direct but can also be indirect—to acknowledge the customers' feedback and to let the customer provide them with additional information on how they perceive the experience could be improved. Responding to the customer in such a way may not fix every problem, but it does let the customer know that someone is really listening.

As much as responding to the customer as part of a customer experience program is essential to ensuring the customer is acknowledged as being heard, it is often an afterthought within the Customer Experience measurement platforms. One of the software platforms provided end-to-end tools with a systematic approach to the workflow. Another provided tools to identify the concern behind the concern when speaking with the customer. One of the more popular platforms only had a system to notify the frontline manager in the event of a customer complaint. All have some element of allowing the brand to "close the loop" with the customer, yet none had the ability to do all three of those processes just described. This is true when I look across all the Customer Experience survey platforms I used prior to my current role. Some had tactical tools, few had strategic tools for the frontline, none had linked the two sufficiently.

Even when getting it right, sometimes brands (and the Customer Experience software providers that serve them) still get it wrong—using templated responses instead of responding with an empathetic note. Even worse, was arguing with a customer during the resolution process instead of simply acknowledging that a mistake was made and apologizing. One of the more sophisticated software providers gives brands the ability to put everything on "cruise control"—automating every aspect of the data collection, the triggering of a closed-loop feedback ticket, and then just automating the response to the customer—setting the status to "resolved" without anyone having reviewing the negative feedback isolated from the full set of responses.

I have often cited an example of a car rental company that I used in the same airport station every week for three years. Every week upon returning the vehicle, I would be asked to complete a survey before I ever received my email receipt. One day, I had a negative experience upon returning the vehicle, so I decided to let them know. Immediately after pressing "submit," I received an apology email—supposedly from the manager of the rental car station—and a coupon for my next visit to that specific station. This provided little benefit to me since I had to use the company rate to rent and it did not allow coupons added to the fact that I was unlikely to take a vacation in the location where I was working every week. I decided to assess the system—every week a negative response, every week a coupon with the same templated response. This continued for several months until my job took me to another location. It was a few months later that someone finally reached out to me, not to ask me for my feedback, but to try to understand why I was no longer renting from them. This was no love story.

Beyond the platforms, all the terminology and lingo associated with Customer Experience management practices all speak about "action" relative to actionable insights, but never really force the idea of acting with the customer. The literature and publications often focus on the analytics and the proper motivations of those tasked with improving or enhancing the Customer Experience. In fact, asking a popular Generative AI platform about "what types of actions should a company take when using a Customer Experience platform" left me unimpressed with the results.

> *Implementing a Customer Experience (CX) measurement program is just the first step; <u>acting</u> on the insights gained from it is crucial for improving customer satisfaction and loyalty. Here are some key <u>actions</u> a company should take based on the findings of its CX measurement program:*

1. ***Identify Areas for Improvement****: Use the data collected from the CX program to pinpoint specific areas where the customer experience can be enhanced. This might include analyzing customer feedback, identifying pain points in the customer journey, and understanding areas of dissatisfaction.*

2. ***Set Clear Objectives****: Establish clear, <u>actionable</u> objectives for improving the customer experience based on the insights gathered. These objectives should be specific, measurable, achievable, relevant, and time-bound (SMART).*

3. ***Prioritize <u>Actionable</u> Insights****: Not all insights will require immediate attention. Prioritize the insights that have the greatest impact on customer satisfaction and loyalty, as well as those that align with the company's strategic goals.*

4. ***Implement Changes****: Take concrete <u>actions</u> to address the identified areas for improvement. This might involve changes to products, services, processes, policies, or employee training. Ensure that these changes are communicated effectively to both customers and employees.*

5. ***Monitor Progress****: Continuously monitor the impact of the changes implemented through the CX program. Track key metrics related to customer satisfaction, loyalty, retention, and advocacy to gauge progress over time.*

6. ***Iterate and Adapt****: The customer experience is an ongoing journey, so it's important to continuously iterate and adapt based on customer feedback and changing market dynamics. Regularly review and update the CX measurement program to ensure its relevance and effectiveness.*

7. ***Empower Employees****: Equip frontline employees with the tools, training, and autonomy they need to deliver exceptional customer experiences. Empowered employees who can respond effectively to customer needs can have a significant impact on overall satisfaction and loyalty.*

8. ***Promote a Customer-Centric Culture****: Foster a culture within the organization that prioritizes the needs and preferences of customers. Encourage cross-functional collaboration and alignment around the goal of delivering outstanding customer experiences.*

9. ***Seek Feedback****: Actively solicit feedback from customers on an ongoing basis to ensure that their evolving needs and expectations are being met. Use a variety of feedback channels, such as surveys, interviews, social media, and online reviews, to gather insights from diverse perspectives.*

10. ***Celebrate Successes****: Recognize and celebrate achievements and milestones in improving the customer experience. Positive reinforcement can help sustain momentum and motivation across the organization.*

> *By taking these <u>actions</u>, a company can leverage its CX measurement program to drive meaning-*
> *ful improvements in customer satisfaction, loyalty, and ultimately, business success.*

As these Generative AI tools improve, we may see a different answer some day, but the response generated in this example used "action" and its variations without any reference to speaking to the customer. Perhaps the closest example is where it suggests that the brand should "seek feedback" from customers in the form of surveys, but rarely talks about recovery from a negative experience. This response is certainly missing an element of empathy that we might expect from a machine response.

Understanding Journeys—Taking Actions

I hold a philosophy that improvements can be made to the Customer Experience by using these two steps: understanding journeys and taking actions. Using Customer Experience to act should be at the heart of any program, platform, or initiative. While it is easy to get distracted by the steps that it takes to launch and maintain an initiative as complex as a Customer Experience program, it is important that every program should refocus on the primary goal—take actions that positively impact the Customer Experience to continue to attract and retain the types of customers the brands desire.

There is more than one way to act. There is the simple method of responding individually to the feedback received from customers—during a survey or through another mechanism. Just a quick search online of "ticketing systems" resulted in seventeen sponsored hyperlinks to such software tools—none of which were associated with Customer Experience management technology. One unique aspect of ticketing systems within Customer Experience platforms is that, in addition to operational and sales data that might be added to an individual record, each response will include opinions—about the brand, service or product. The conversation has already begun with the customer, and it is important to acknowledge and respond.

Within these platforms, it is generally considered to be a "closed-loop feedback" tool. Following a survey, get notified about the results, review results, begin a conversation with the customer, resolve the customer's concern and close the ticket. This process can be undertaken for any number of reasons following a survey— most often for a negative response to an overall key performance indicator from the survey. However, reasons can include a negative response to a key initiative (a specific score about a product is low despite many recent efforts to improve the product), a specific item the customer desired was not available for purchase at the time of the survey, or simply a customer indicating they would like to be contacted. More sophisticated systems could also identify keywords in an open end (such as "lawsuit") and route a ticket to the appropriate department for the proper attention. It may not just be about detractor recovery, it may also represent an opportunity to improve operations, recognize an employee or even close a sale where appropriate.

The workflow for closed-loop ticketing can even provide a brand with opportunities to promote themselves. If a customer indicates that they had extraordinary service with the brand, you can use ticketing to ask a customer to write a review through a personalized response to the ticket. This is quite different from pushing them to a review website after a survey because the automated layer is removed and a conversation begins.

Another missed opportunity in many closed-loop feedback systems is evaluating the feedback from a customer following the intervention by the brand. Consider the car rental example provided previously. Without direct knowledge of the inner workings of the program in place there, I am left to assume that there was an incentive for either "closing" tickets or the speed at which they were closed. If anyone had asked for my feedback following each ticket being marked as resolved, they would have found that my satisfaction with the company decreased due to this less-than-personalized approach to my situation. Without overwhelming the customer, simply ask how satisfied they are now following resolution, what I call a WinBack survey.

Taking You for Another Loop

Insights are good, but action is better. However, with all the focus on the "latest and greatest" dashboard widget, a remarkably simple analysis is often overlooked—or not done at all because of the limitations of the closed-loop feedback platform. That is understanding the root cause of every ticket that is presented within the system. Tagging these closed-loop tickets and providing this type of insight can help an organization improve scaling up.

Originally introduced in a concept by Bain & Company as part of the Net Promoter Score system, the concept of Inner Loop and Outer Loop focused on actions at multiple levels. The Inner Loop—often referred to as a closed loop, was really about a response to an individual customer—taking actions to improve that individual's situation, a very tactical approach using customer alerts along with detractors and promoter ticketing. Time to action was expected to be immediate, often initiated by a frontline manager or employee, with a caveat of responding to the right customers—those that are beneficial to the brand, with less focus on the "serial complainers."

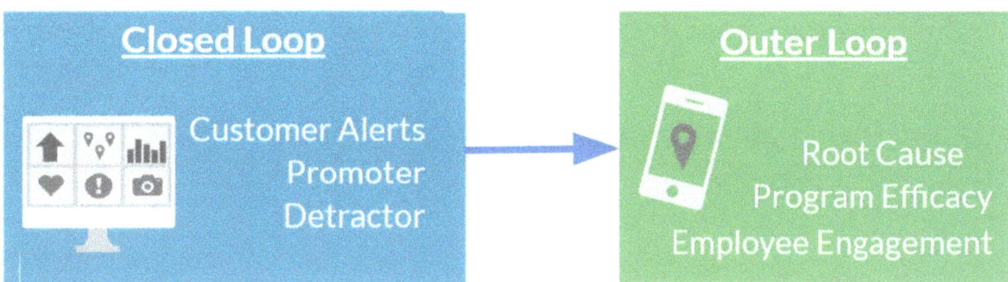

The introduction of the Outer Loop is about focusing on strategic improvements that would be initiated at a higher level within the organization. Instead of one day or one week turnaround times, such initiatives would be planned to take place over the course of weeks or even months. However, to decide which initiatives should be leveraged by an organization, there needs to be an analysis of the pervasiveness of the problem, the return on investment of fixing the situation, and management buy-in toward pushing for a remedy.

In a simple example, consider a company that delivers appliances to households. Each delivery is scheduled on a certain day and within a time window provided to the customer. Following each delivery, suppose the survey shows several upset customers on an ongoing basis complaining about missed delivery times. Of course, each of those customers should be contacted with an empathic and genuine response consistent with the closed-loop feedback process. However, continually apologizing to individual customers will not really fix what is behind the problem—the root cause.

In taking actions to resolve such issues, the conversations with customers should include an understanding of where the process collapsed. Was the scheduling system offering times that were not available? Were the distances between deliveries too great to meet the promised delivery windows? Are there not enough trucks or delivery drivers? Are delays happening on site at the customer location?

Digging deeper than just the overall problem and understanding the root causes impacting that score will allow brands to act. It is more than just stating a problem and defining a plan. It should include defining the team that will support the initiative, and understanding the tasks to complete the missions, metrics, and KPIs that will be used to evaluate success and key milestones where upper management can be kept informed. Many Customer Experience platforms provide a template or an offline tool to accomplish this but, to keep individuals accountable, it should be built into the technology of the Customer Experience management system. The teams tasked with such initiatives should be cross-functional, have access to the data they need to evaluate the problem more closely and the ability to act on the tasks and results arising from the work.

Using CX to Act

Undertaking a new Customer Experience program or bringing on a new Customer Experience management platform is a huge action by any organization. But simply launching and deploying a new survey will not positively affect the Customer Experience. In fact, there is more risk that it will harm the image of the company if nothing substantially is done by the brand to improve CX based on the feedback. Actions taken should be beneficial to the customer by improving the experience and beneficial to the organization through increased loyalty, lifetime value, or operational efficiency. An added benefit is that providing the tools necessary to make a customer happy will also benefit the employees that directly serve them where they are empowered to make things right with the customer. Insights may lead to areas of potential improvement, but only appropriate actions—whether through Closed Loop or Outer Loop workflows—will benefit the brand long term.

Chapter 11—Networking and Professional Advancement

Greg Melia, CAE

> *"Professionals thrive when they can learn from and collaborate with other like-minded individuals. When you join an association, you're aligning with others like yourself who are striving for the best."*
>
> **Karl Sharicz, HorizonCX**

Chances are that "customer experience professional" was not your career aspiration when you were a child—not likely as a college student or even in your first professional job. Customer experience is still a young career field and most CX professionals have discovered this wonderful, meaningful career by accidental luck or as a natural evolution of their innate customer-focused thinking. I feel especially honored to write this very needed chapter to provide you with things to consider to help you plan to have a long and an accomplished career in customer experience leadership now that you have chosen CX as a career aspiration.

Getting Started—What Is Customer Experience Anyway?

Let me begin with a story. Years ago, when I was working as Director of Certification for an association, I was asked at a wedding reception what I did for a living. I responded that I was a certification manager, which was met with dumbfounded stares, which continued when I tried to explain associations. Searching for a point of connection, I asked, "Do you have a CPA help you prepare your taxes?" The person answered affirmatively, and I explained that CPA is an example of a certification that is granted by an association, and that I did similar work for people who run associations. I thought for a moment that my analogy had worked until they asked, "Oh, so you can help me with my taxes?" I offered a harmless lie, stating that I wasn't authorized to give advice in Ohio and excused myself from the conversation.

Chances are you are going to have to explain your career at some point—and because customer experience isn't especially well-known, you may encounter a similar difficulty unless you are better prepared. So, the first way to make sure you can effectively network for professional advancement is to make sure that you are able to describe customer experience and the role of customer experience professionals.

The Customer Experience Professionals Association (CXPA) is the professional association for the CX community. It defines Customer Experience (CX) as "the perception that customers have of an organization—one that is formed based on interactions across all touchpoints, people, and technology over time." Customer Experience is more than just customer service (which tends to focus on the often-reactionary moments in which a customer interacts with an organization), customer success (which is often the post-sales onboarding and renewal processes for customers), customer loyalty (which often focuses squarely on recognizing and upselling existing customers), or customer relations (which often serves as the public interface with potential and existing customers). Customer Experience is more holistic, including each of the aforementioned factors but also including customer understanding, design, analytics, and collaborative leadership to ensure that the customer's journey of discovery, interaction, and commerce with an organization create positive perceptions at every step. This is a business discipline used by organizations like Amazon, Apple, The Ritz-Carlton, Nordstrom, and Southwest Airlines as a competitive advantage that drives customer loyalty, market share, and sustainable business success.

CXPA further defines a CX professional as "a catalyst who enhances an organization's results by understanding, designing, and improving experiences across the entire customer relationship." This is because unlike a position charged with executing a specific task over which they have complete control (such as a retail cashier who is solely tasked with executing the experience in the store checkout lane; an accounts payable specialist who is responsible for vendor payment management; or a contact center representative that is charged with the task of handling customer inquiries and complaints) the customer experience professional works across the organization by influencing departments and aligning their tasks to create an overall experience flow that meets or exceeds customer expectations.

Getting comfortable with understanding and describing your role as a customer experience professional is a great first step in preparing for networking. It is likely that you will use a less formal definition than what I have presented above for informal, social conversations — such as "I work to ensure that my company is meeting and exceeding customer needs" or "I help our organization be customer obsessed so that our customers are raving fans of our company." However, you should also be prepared for a more formal description to use in organized professional networking events such as university organized symposiums. Being more advanced and specific in your description will help others to draw connections to those in their network with whom you will benefit.

Building a Broad and Solid Foundation

Customer experience can be an isolated and challenging role because you are sometimes the only person in a conversation (or even within your organization) that is representing the voice of the customer and advocating for a change in the way that business is done. That's why it's especially important that CX professionals build a broad solid foundation of knowledge and connections to help support them through the inevitable challenges they'll face within their career. As one senior CX leader once remarked to me, CX can feel like you are pushing a rock up a hill. When you build relationships with others, it may not make the work much easier, but at least you have company as you push the rock together.

Building relationships should be more than collecting contact information or LinkedIn connections—it should be about getting to know and understand others. What motivates them? What are their preferences? What irritates them the most? What are their aspirations for the future? Take time to get to know and connect on a human level, learning about their career path, pets, family, values, and beliefs. This will create stronger relationships that will make a substantial difference overall.

A natural place to start building your support network is to begin within your organization. Employ the advice from the previous paragraph and remember to build relationships with people at every level of the organization. Seek to build a broad network first, then prioritize developing deeper relationships with those who show early promise in helping you grow within your career.

The next natural place to grow your network is within your region or industry. These are individuals who may be able to provide insight based on your shared characteristics. In reaching out to establish relationships with these individuals, it is often helpful to begin from a place of honesty and genuine curiosity. For example, you could reach out to someone at a similar organization who holds the same title as you by sending a note like this: "I'm the CX director at Acme Corp and I wanted to reach out because of a challenge that I'm facing. I wonder if you have encountered this and whether you have any advice. Would you be open to a quick call or a coffee?" LinkedIn is a great resource for making this type of outreach, or you may be able to connect through CXPA or to another CX group.

It is worth noting that the CX community is regularly active on LinkedIn, so you will not have any difficulty finding other CX professionals, groups in which to engage, or content producers to follow. There always seems to be CX news, discussions or online events happening, with content ranging from novice to advanced, and from verified facts to individual opinions. I'll cover how you can better assess which sources to trust later in this chapter, but as you engage on LinkedIn, do keep in mind that your participation on LinkedIn becomes a portion of your own professional identity. Avoid making posts that may be perceived as uneducated, inappropriate, or unprofessional. Manage yourself with grace and empathy.

Getting Trusted Help

It is wise for you to ensure that you are learning and getting support from experienced CX professionals that you can trust. Here are a few ideas to get started.

- Establish a mentoring relationship with one or more CX professionals who are in positions to which you aspire.
- Participate in a professionally coached or self-organized small group of CX professionals who share common professional advancement interests. (*One word of caution:* self-organized small groups are highly dependent on the composition of the group and its self-managed effort to work together. For that reason, a professional coach who can add experience and assist with accountability is often desirable.)
- Retain an individual professional coach.
- Join a professional CX association. Associations bring together motivated members to exchange ideas, support one another, and provide resources to help you succeed. There are an increasing number of CX associations from which to choose. Chances are that if you plan a lengthy career in CX, you'll likely join more than one CX association during your career and often more than one at the same time. The Customer Experience Professionals Association (CXPA), the global association for the customer experience professional community, can be found on the web at cxpaglobal.org.

Choose a Knowledge Framework

If you do not have formal training in CX, it is important for you to take an intentional and proactive approach to building your customer experience knowledge.

The term customer experience first emerged in the mid-1990s and is now widely used. However, that does not mean that that it is well understood. Just as it is important to have a firm understanding of the definition of customer experience, it is also important to adopt a framework to guide your customer experience knowledge development. There are frameworks developed by software providers, management consulting firms, and individual thought leaders. My preference is the CXPA CX Framework because of the process that was used to create it.

The CXPA CX Framework was developed based on an industry-wide job task analysis that was conducted by the CXPA in 2013 and updated in 2020. As part of this process, in 2020, more than 300 customer experience professionals provided feedback on the importance of job tasks covering the scope of the CX profession. The core competencies for CX were identified through the results of this analysis. Within each competency, specific job tasks and key knowledge, skill, and ability areas were further identified. The core competencies in the CXPA CX Framework are Customer Insights and Understanding; Customer Experience Strategy; Metrics, Measurements, and ROI; Design, Implementation, and Innovation; and Culture and Accountability.

The CXPA CX Framework is a broad, general rubric. It does not require that you use a specific tool, technique, or metric—instead, it is focused on helping ensure that you address all critical elements of a successful CX program when choosing the collection of tools, techniques, and metrics that best fit your organization's circumstances.

Once you have chosen a high-level framework, you will have a new lens to evaluate the resources to build your knowledge as discussed in the next section. You will have a new assessment tool to determine how a course or book fits into the big picture and whether it is comprehensive. This is important because it is easy to get enamored by what is said in a slick presentation or by an engaging speaker—while overlooking essential elements that are omitted. Here's another truth: CX only works when each part of the CX program works … an omission or breakdown can cause the entire CX to come crashing down.

Build Your Knowledge

There are many resources available nowadays to build your CX knowledge, available in a wide variety of formats and price points, including a considerable number of free resources. In choosing the resources in which to invest time and money, keep your end goal in mind: what will help me improve my CX understanding and leadership skills to deliver better results for my organization and advance my career?

An effective way to make sure you focus on getting the results you need is to assess your current knowledge against the framework that you have selected. Read each of the outlined statements in the framework and give yourself a self-assessment, in these categories:

0) I do not know what this means.
1) I know what this means but I am not 100% sure.
2) I know what this means but have never had formal training in it.
3) I am skilled at this, through training or successful experience.
4) I am an expert in this task.

This simple self-assessment can help you identify what knowledge gaps to address, as well as to select resources that address the topic at the level appropriate to your knowledge.

Association Laboratory Inc. conducted a survey in early 2024 that asked CX professionals across the globe about the resources they use for professional advancement. They found that most CX professionals use more than one source for their knowledge development, but no one knowledge source is routinely used by all CX professionals. The primary survey findings are shown in the figure below.

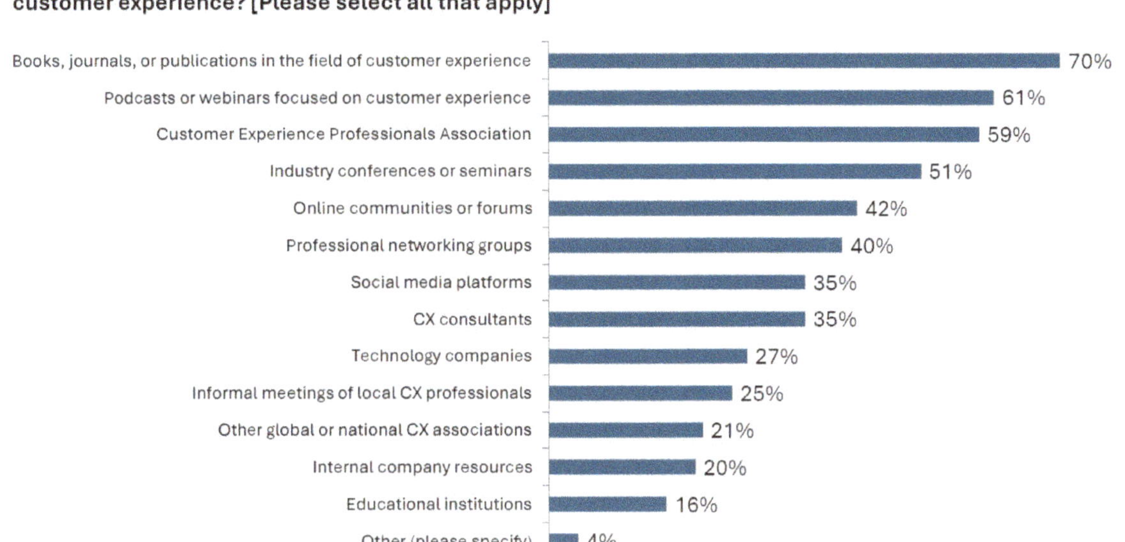

Below are some considerations as you consider knowledge resources.

- **Books and publications** are the most frequently used knowledge-building resource. The CXPA CX Book of Knowledge is the comprehensive consensus CX resource for the field, written, reviewed, and refined by more than 70 contributors. Similar books that feature multiple authors (such as the one you are reading) are often valuable for the multiple perspectives they bring to the field. If choosing a book written by a single author or small author team, consider the qualifications of the authors and the independence of the content—can you trust that the resource reflects wisdom built from CX experience, offered with the intent of knowledge advancement rather than promotion of a specific commercial interest?

- **Podcasts and Webinars** provide free and low-cost convenient options that in many cases are extremely informative. Do look carefully at the experience and motivation of the host. Do they define CX in the same way that you do? Do they have experience and expertise you can trust? Will the session give sufficient insight that you will be able to apply in your organization or career? Look for program hosts that push beyond entertainment to draw out insights rather than just offering engaging interviews or celebrity guests.

- **Formal or informal CX associations or networking groups**—After books, podcasts, and webinars, CX professionals reported turning to a network of CX peers for knowledge development and community, whether through the CXPA, online communities, or other networking groups. In choosing the community that is right for you, consider both how the organization aligns with the CX framework you have chosen and whether you feel welcome and connected to the group. Keep open to the fact that in many cases, you may be well served by participating in multiple groups.

- **Formal Training through industry conference or educational institutions**—Just over half of the respondents reported using industry conferences and seminars for education, and just under one in seven turned to educational institutions for learning. Formal training is likely to provide the deepest dive on general topics. Look at the credentials of the faculty, listed learning outcomes, and previous student reviews to make sure that you are investing time and resources wisely. Another key consideration is with whom you will be learning. When possible, seek to take courses with others at a similar stage of knowledge that you discovered in your self-assessment.

- **CX Consultants and Technology Companies**—Consultants and technology companies can be especially valuable because of their in-depth expertise and experience across multiple clients. However, you should be sure to consider their experience and ethos. For example, it may make sense to seek training from an individual who has worked solely with one technology company if your goal is strictly focused on use of that company's product—but if you are seeking a broader understanding of a topic including the variety of potential technology partners, that same exclusive experience may be a limitation. Also, look at the ethos or character of the provider. Are they known for their willingness to share? Are they active and respected in the CX community? An effective way to find the right partners is to ask for a complimentary initial conversation and see how you feel about the way the conversation unfolds, especially regarding the priorities for next steps. Choose partners that treat you as a professional partner, not a sales target.

Demonstrate Leadership and Get Recognition

If you want to be a CX leader, you need others to see you as a CX leader too. Within your organization, be proactive about volunteering to take on new assignments that will help you build and demonstrate your skills and leadership. Offer to be on a team, manage a project, or even lead an initiative. During the new assignment, develop new relationships with those around you—both by asking for their mentorship and in getting to know the strengths of your colleagues.

Beyond your organization, author articles or case studies about your CX initiatives, be a guest speaker at a college or university, or volunteer within a CX association. Each of these allows you to organize and present your thoughts at the same time as demonstrating your CX advancement.

Strong consideration should also be given to earning professional certificates, degrees, or certifications. These credentials are objective, external validations of your CX knowledge. They help to make the case that you have specialized CX knowledge, and they can help to differentiate you from similar candidates without such qualifications. Professional certificates indicate the completion of a specified set of courses and may include additional steps such as passing a quiz to verify your comprehension. Higher education degrees indicate satisfactory completion of a rigorous collection of courses and assessment by professional faculty. They represent a significant investment of time, tuition, and effort. Professional certifications typically include educational and experience requirements, a rigorous exam, and ongoing maintenance requirements. Each can play a role in your CX journey, and it is not unusual to see CX professionals within multiple credentials.

The most respected and prominent professional certification in the CX field is the Certified Customer Experience Professional (CCXP). It is valued by CX professionals, employers, and governmental entities because it is designed by industry peers, grounded in industry research, and administered by the CXPA, the independent global association for the CX profession. It is smart to look at the requirements of the CCXP early in your career and develop a plan to put yourself in position to earn the CCXP when you are ready and eligible to do so. Adopting the CXPA CX framework to guide your development is a great first step, followed by taking on assignments within your organization or volunteering to help you gain experience in each of the five competencies that will put you on a track to fulfill the application requirements. Choosing books and education programs offered by those who have earned the CCXP or otherwise aligned with the CXPA CX framework helps ensure that the content you are being taught aligns with the CCXP. When you are ready to apply, if you want training tailored to preparing for the exam, CXPA's Recognized Training Providers are an option for you.

There are also numerous individual and organization award programs available to the CX community, and when chosen wisely, they can be a value-added recognition. When executed professionally, these programs require a well-organized application that includes sufficient data to objectively compare award applicants. A credible program should be transparent about the factors used in evaluation, and it should have a collection of judges that are skilled and respected for their integrity. Most importantly, the entire process should be free from self-interest and undue influence. When the aforementioned factors are met, such awards can be a piece of adding external validation to your individual or team accomplishments. However, there have also been awards and recognitions that do not meet these expectations. Here are some red flags to watch out for.

- You are contacted to let you know you have won an award, subject to your agreement to pay for a promotional package.
- Recognition is granted without you or someone else having applied.
- There is an explicit or implicit expectation that award recipients will promote the sponsor of the awards program.
- The staff of the granting organization solely judges the awards.
- The award selection criteria are not credible (e.g., declaring someone a CX thought leader based solely on their volume of social media posts or followers, regardless of the content of such posts)

When you notice these types of red flags, it is wise to proceed with caution. An award ties your individual brand to the sponsoring organization. Make sure that elevates (rather than detracts) from your credibility.

Manage Your Career—Don't Let it Manage You.

CX can be an incredibly special and rewarding career—but it is also one with many twists and turns. Chances are you will hold a variety of roles with a variety of organizations over the course of your career. Recognize this from the outset and position yourself for success regardless of the circumstances around you. Here are a few tips.

1) **Make sure that you schedule a periodic career development check-in.** Whether this is a self-reflection opportunity or with a peer, mentor, or coach, you should make time at least once a year to revisit your knowledge against the CX framework of your choosing; the experience, opportunities, and knowledge that you have accumulated; and readiness for next steps in your career. Use this to update your proactive career development plan for the coming year. (Note: this should be a personal reflection outside of your employee performance review.)

2) **Document your accomplishments along the way.** Speak, write, or submit applications to respected award programs to help you organize, document, and tell the story of your CX development. Keep your resume and LinkedIn profile up to date.

3) **Remain open to conversations and opportunities.** Keep your eyes open for emerging opportunities to take on additional responsibilities within or outside your organization. There is a saying in the creative problem-solving community that the best way to have a great idea is to have lots of ideas. In the same spirit, the best way to find great opportunities for advancement is to consider lots of opportunities.

4) **Be prepared to be resilient.** Even the best, tenured CX professional will experience trying times and emotional setbacks. Be mentally and emotionally prepared that you will too. In those times, let the career development steps you have taken and professional network you have fostered help you get back on the path to success.

Best wishes to you for a long and productive CX career. Please know that I and the CXPA community are here to support you.

Chapter 12—Customer Progress Design (jobs-to-be-done)

Eckhart Boehme

> *"When we buy a product, we essentially 'hire' something to get a job done. If it does the job well, when we are confronted with the same job, we hire that same product again."*
> **Clayton Christensen**

Your Mission: Helping Customers Make Progress

Helping customers improve their lives is one of the greatest services organizations can provide. Hence, focusing on improving the status quo, meaning refining, or fixing existing products or services, is not enough to unlock the full potential of value creation. Helping people to improve their lives or businesses also offers great growth opportunities for your company. This is reason enough to look at how contributing to progress can be done most effectively.

If we want to delight customers beyond the products and services they already use, we need to help them change and adopt new ones that meet their needs better than before. To do this, we…

- must understand what unmet needs exist,
- get a sense of which need fulfillment will make a positive contribution to our business,
- understand how we could help customers most effectively acquire new products or services,
- and finally help customers realize the promised benefits.

In short, we need to help customers master their "journey to improvement" so that it makes a difference in their lives and at the same time helps our company grow profitably. This undertaking can be divided into two parts (1) doing the right things for the customer and the organization and (2) doing things the right way by creating the right value propositions and experiences.

In recent years, the so-called Job to Be Done (JTBD) theory, popularized by Harvard Business School Professor Clayton Christensen, emerged as an effective tool to guide us in "doing the right things." This theory argues that customers "hire" your product or service to get a job done. They try to achieve a specific outcome in a certain circumstance.

What we subsequently try to understand are…

- the specific jobs that customers are trying to get done,
- the significance of these jobs,
- the potential to relieve their pains and to improve the results related to these jobs.

These factors help us decide what value-add we could create for customers. In addition, assessing the business potential for each "customer job," will help us not only to do the right things but decide what customer "job" will provide the greatest business potential. While it is crucial to understand how customers want to improve their lives or businesses, the breakthroughs to innovative customer experiences are often—unarticulated—insights into what desired outcome they are looking for.

A Holistic View of the Customer

Organizations most effectively align with customers when all customer-facing activities are centered around the same customer job and are targeted at helping customers move with ease through their customer journey. To get clarity on what product, marketing, and sales strategies are most useful, we developed several mental models that help understand what triggers customers to move to the next phase and what support customers need in each phase of the customer journey to complete it successfully.

Introducing Customer Progress Design

Customer Progress Design® (CPD) is a method for developing a customer-centric strategy. CPD is based on the principles of the Jobs to Be Done (JTBD) theory that aims at understanding why customers pull new products into their lives.

CPD helps to develop an overall strategy that supports human beings in making progress in their personal life or in a business context. This strategy consists of solutions (products, services, brands, etc.) as well as marketing, communication, and buying aids that help them to satisfy their desire for progression. With the help of this integrated approach, deep, targeted, and relevant insights are achieved. They can be ultimately translated into strategies for serving existing and new markets, meaning clusters of "customer jobs." In doing so, CPD helps organizations stay relevant to existing customers and facilitates bringing in new ones.

These benefits are made possible by using the desired improvements in life or in business as a starting point for ideas, for innovations, and as a basis for marketing campaigns. Furthermore, this integrated approach promotes collaboration between the different functions within the company. A universal picture of the need for progress is always at the center of the analysis.

The following insight serves as the basis of our method: people set out on a journey to seek progress when they need improvement. Contrary to what most organizations believe, customers aren't looking to buy their product… they are looking to "hire" a solution to get a job better done.[6] Since in most cases people need external help to do this, insights into the need for progress are of utmost importance.

If a company's development and marketing activities are oriented toward enabling people to progress in life, then they have a clear organizational purpose. This purpose benefits customers as well as suppliers. The fundamental motive of CPD is to enable people to progress, not to manipulate their behavior. This is expressed by the CPD's principle that customers should always be able to act in a self-determined and conscious way.

The Four Phases of Customer Progress Design

In the Customer Progress Design[7] model, human beings make progress in cycles. Once they notice that they need improvement they enter a phase of "passive search" where they become aware of the need to act. In the second phase, they actively search for a new solution. Often, this phase is exploratory because customers at the beginning of their journey are not familiar with the solution space. Sometimes they even have the challenge to articulate what they are looking for and or don't know the exact terms of the solution(s) they have in mind.

---

6   Clayton Christensen et. al., *Competing Against Luck* by Harper Collins, 2016

7   For details see unipro-solutions.com

In the third phase, when they find a set of appropriate products or services, they need to compare them and decide which one is most appropriate and provides the best value for the money. In the fourth phase, after they have acquired the "new way of doing it," they experience the new solution and assess their success. If the acquisition were successful, they would keep it and build a new habit. If not, they may return it, acquire something new, or go back to their old behavior.

These phases are triggered by events. Something happens in the life of an individual that causes him or her to move to the next phase of the cycle: a first thought makes them feel a deficit, so they look passively for a new solution. Perhaps they procrastinate. A trigger event makes them then enter an "active search." Maybe he or she got inspired by a new product, or something happened that increased their "pain." In this phase, they also may make up their mind about what they want to achieve in a new situation and what to avoid. Yet another trigger event may cause them to consider specific products or services. This trigger could be a "roadblock" that disappeared or one that increased their pain. Sometimes there are even trigger events for buying a product at a certain time.

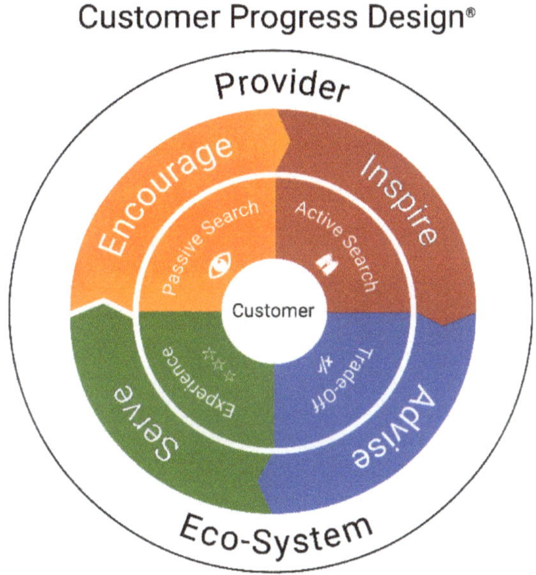

Figure 1: Customer Progress Design flywheel.

As providers, we can help customers make progress by providing help in each of the four phases.

True customer-centricity starts with caring about them even before they become customers. Our service as a provider could be helping people end their procrastination. Procrastination has the potential to be harmful or at least create regret about their late start to tackle the issue at hand.

Like the "Just do it"[8] campaign by Nike, one of the most successful advertising campaigns in history. The campaign aimed to address the rising problem of obesity and encouraged the public to get physically active. This is when we as providers can encourage customers to enter their customer journey and stop postponing.

---

8   https://medium.com/@dimitrios.kales/just-do-it-the-secret-story-behind-the-worlds-most-recognisable-slogan-7736d901d8ef

In the active search phase, we can help customers to explore the solution space. Our job is to inspire them and consider the "new." There could be vastly different solution categories that fulfill that need. We can help customers form their opinion by providing orientation as to what the solution space could look like. Examples of services are self-assessments, questionnaires, checklists, consulting services, or any kind of orientation. We can also ensure that our solution is found and considered.

In the trade-off phase, customers look for clarity as to what alternative is the one that best meets the objectives. Customers often like to test-drive offerings to experience first-hand if the solution is a good fit. They also like to buy products or services with the "best value." In this phase, we can also manage objections proactively that the customer may have.

In the fourth phase, customers are looking for a successful execution of their jobs-to-be-done. In this phase, providers need to offer an alternative that is better than the "old way." The sum of the benefits must be greater than the total cost of acquisition and adoption. The experience should be surprisingly good and reinsure them in their purchase.

As providers, we don't need to perform all these services. We have the option to collaborate with other providers in the eco-system that specialize in certain products, services, marketing, or sales disciplines to augment our performances.

Jobs to Be Done for Clarifying Customer Needs

A customer job is the progress that a person wants to make in each circumstance.[9] This presents itself as *a job to be done*. Customer jobs exist at different hierarchical levels: Jobs at a high level describe the progress in life they are seeking. These usually represent an unspoken or subconsciously pursued purpose. Jobs on a low "altitude" consist of specific task and lead into the "jobs" above.[10]

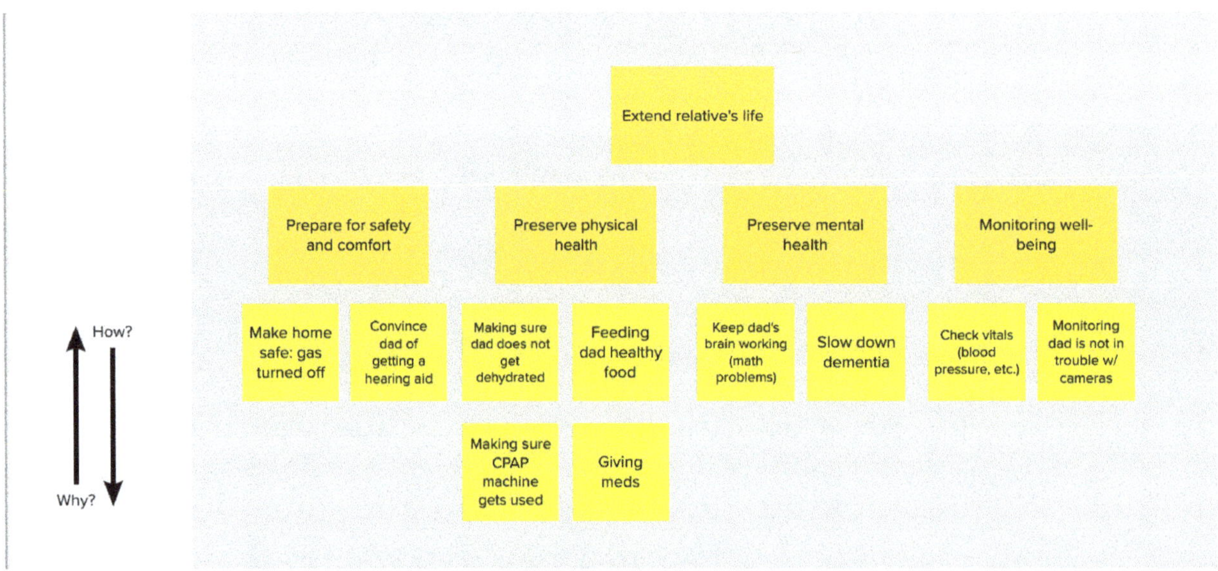

Figure 2: Customer Job Map

---

9   Clayton Christensen et. al., Competing Against Luck by Harper Collins, 2016

10   Jim Kalbach, The Jobs to be done Playbook by Two Waves Books, 2020

Realizing the customer's job at the highest level is important to keep an eye on the intended progress and not get lost in the details of a task. The objective is to find out what purpose a customer wants to pursue but may not be able to articulate. Knowing customer jobs at a low level enables us to realize them technically.

A customer job can have one of the following *dimensions* or a combination of them:[11]

Functional
A functional job relates to the factual performance of a functional task or factual solution of a problem.
- E. g. getting from A to B, calculating a value, or getting registered for an event.

Emotional
An emotional customer job refers to a person seeking emotional satisfaction or fulfillment.
- E. g. enjoying oneself or obtaining peace of mind.

Social
A social customer job refers to the tasks or goals related to social interactions, connections, and relationships.
- E. g. Getting recognition or feeling well by helping others.

Consumers and business customers usually try to pursue combinations of these jobs, such as transporting a delicate good from one place to another and having the peace of mind that it arrives at its destination on time and intact. It is crucial to understand which jobs or job combinations customers try to get done.

The 12 Elements of Customer Progress Design
To make better business decisions, we will need data from customers about their "journey to progress;" customers who acquired a new product or service, tried a workaround, or compensated for a deficiency. Asking hypothetical questions like future actions or intentions is of little value and can even be misleading. This data is usually not available in databases or on the internet. We can gather it by doing thoughtful customer interviews. We can investigate the buying journey of consumers or business buyers. We can find out about their experience with a product or in a job role. There are many topics that we should investigate to understand customers holistically.

In our model, we look for specific factors and we call them "The 12 Elements of Customer Progress Design" to understand customer progress.

---

11   https://hbr.org/2016/09/know-your-customers-jobs-to-be-done

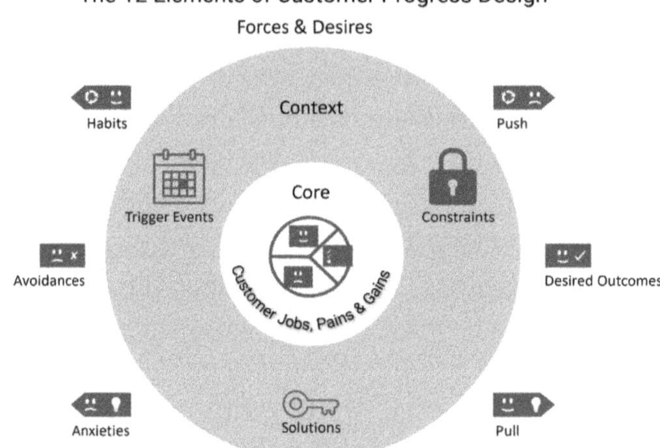

Figure 3: Customer Progress Design Mental and Data Model

Practical Tools and Process

To facilitate customer-centric strategy development and the gathering of data about "customer progress" we developed tools and a process called Customer Progress Design. One of our tools, The Wheel of Progress® helps collect data about customer journeys from customer interviews. It is a visual help that allows customer researchers to capture and structure the responses from the interviewee.

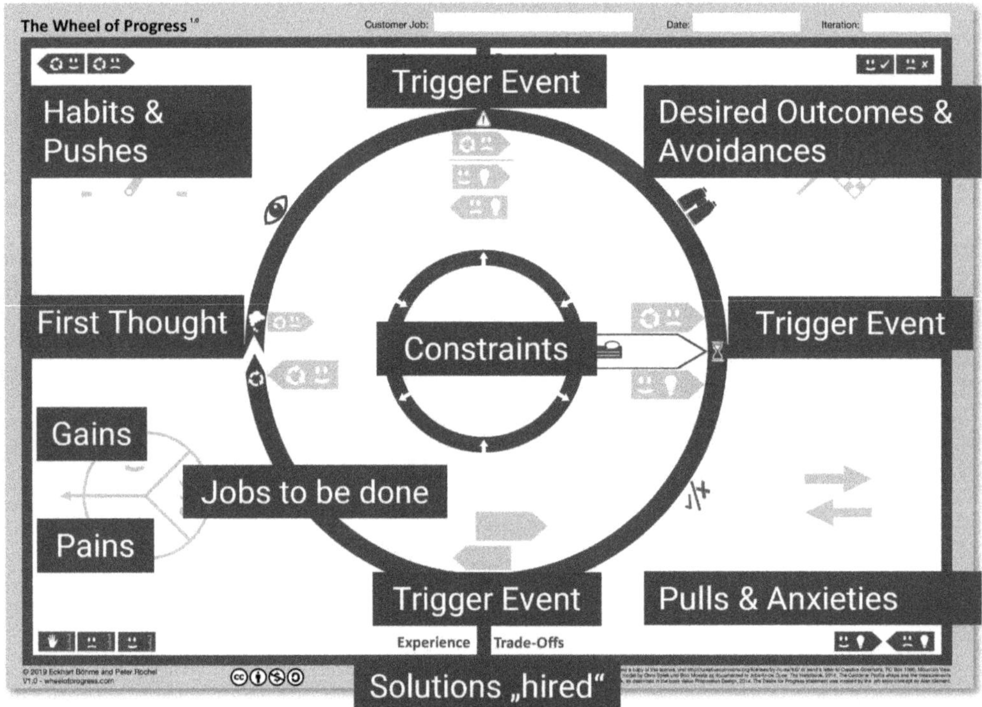

Figure 4: The Wheel of Progress

To find out what the "journey to progress" for a customer looked like, we examined certain characteristics (elements) of progress-making within the cycle. This data helps us to learn about the nature of customer jobs, the context in which customers strived for progress, and psychological forces. The sum of all variables characterizes the sometimes-rocky road to improvement.

In our process, the data from several customer interviews will be evaluated, clustered, and generalized. To help focus on underserved customer jobs, jobs will be prioritized using rational criteria. Prioritized customer jobs and select aggregate data will be used to feed a strategy canvas that helps to ideate strategies for the four phases of customer progress. In this chapter, we can only cover the method at a high level.

Figure 5: The Customer Progress Design Process

Conclusion

To provide a great customer experience, it is important to be empathetic and optimize existing products and practices. However, making the biggest impact on customers' lives takes place when we help them to change and make progress with new solutions. The unprecedented clarity of understanding customer needs that the Jobs to Be Done theory provides, is an enabler for developing products, services, marketing messages, and buying aids, that truly make a difference in people's lives by helping them to move to a better place easier. Focusing on jobs-to-be-done shifts the focus from an offerings-based perspective to a true customer-centric perspective. Making customer progress the mission, provides a powerful purpose and alignment tool that can serve as a north star for the entire organization.

Chapter 13—Quality Approaches to Customer Experience Management

Alec N. Dalton

> *"Quality is never an accident; it is always the result of high intention, sincere effort, intelligent direction and skillful execution; it represents the wise choice of many alternatives."*
>
> **William A. Foster**

Introduction

Whether by design or by default, all customer experiences exhibit a degree of quality … or a lack thereof. As a CX leader, you share responsibility for the design, development, and delivery of quality experiences. This chapter recommends several frameworks that you can use to elevate your quality strategy. We begin by distinguishing three objectives of quality: compliance, competitiveness, and customer-centricity. Then, we explore the Shewhart/Deming Cycle—a powerful sequence for activating the critical functions of quality planning, control, assurance, and improvement. Many tools and techniques are recommended along the way, so you can turn insights into strategic action. Altogether, you will gain quality approaches to customer experience management.

Quality Objectives

Before getting ahead of ourselves, we ought to align on what "quality" means. Doing this poses a challenge … and an opportunity. Ask anyone on your team, or your customers, or even your competitors, and you will likely encounter different definitions: assorted words and phrases like "consistent," "reliable," "as expected," "better than others," "good value," and "worth the price" will likely arise. All are valid, and the variety underscores the fact that "quality" means different things to different people. Nearly all definitions of quality can be synthesized, however, within three managerial objectives: compliance, competitiveness, and customer-centricity.

Quality as Compliance

We first consider compliance—not because it is foremost, but because it is foundational. "Compliance" here refers to conformance to organizational standards. The standards a company sets for itself, along with the standards set by government regulators and industry associations, guide internal operations and affect external perceptions of product and service quality.

High, consistent compliance yields many benefits. Within an organization, cost efficiency is achieved through economies of scale: using standardized resources in greater quantities provides bargaining power for better prices, and the use of repeatable processes limits technological complexity while helping employees develop faster expertise. Their collective knowledge can help the organization be perceived for its expertise, too. Clear performance expectations help employees achieve success and remain engaged, and consistent outputs instill customers' confidence in the reliability of the organization. Further, the same processes that drive consistency often detect and eliminate non-value-adding activities and waste: mistakes, rework, breakdowns, inconsistencies, and variations. Altogether, standards can help an organization achieve quality.

Standards take a variety of forms across supply chains and value streams. In quality management, the acronym "SIPOC" is typically used to summarize these sequences of suppliers, inputs, processes, outputs, and customers. Different types of standards are applicable to different elements, summarized in Table 1 and detailed as follows:

- Supplier expectations: From order accuracy to on-time delivery, organizations should expect quality products and services from their vendors. Assurance can be gained through verifications and vetting processes, like requests-for-proposals, samples, client testimonies, and trial periods.
- Input specifications: Whether sourced from external vendors or produced in-house, inputs should consistently match functional, behavioral, and aesthetic requirements. Otherwise, as the saying goes, "Garbage in equals garbage out."
- Process operating procedures: Taking the inputs, employees and technology should consistently adhere to well-defined, repeatable processes.
- Output specifications: As with input specifications, customer-facing products and services should comply with functional, behavioral, and aesthetic requirements. Observations, inspections, and other validations can ensure requirements are satisfied.
- Customer expectations: Just as your organization has expectations of its suppliers, your customers have expectations of you. Expectations can be influenced by your marketing, by word-of-mouth from other customers, and by customers' past personal experiences with your products and those of competitors.

As work-in-process flows through each element of SIPOC, continuing compliance is key to deliver products and services with highest likelihood of meeting (if not exceeding) customer expectations in the end.

Table 1

Common Quality Standards Across Supply Chain Elements

Supply chain element	Quality standard
Suppliers	Expectations
Inputs	Specifications
Processes	Operating procedures
Outputs	Specifications
Customers	Expectations

We established why standards—and compliance thereof—are important. We distinguished between different types of standards. Where do standards originate, though? Organizations can tap several sources to define standards … and to refine them for continuous improvement. Consider these examples:

- Customers: Standards should be crafted to increase the likelihood that target customers will be consistently satisfied. Proactive consumer research can help you detect expectations, and feedback loops inform whether these were met (and whether any expectations have been missed altogether).
- Employees: Internal subject-matter experts and those on the frontlines of production may be primed with ideas for designing and improving the quality of suppliers, inputs, processes, and outputs. Equally, employees with customer contact can convey feedback to the rest of the organization.

- Government regulators: Legislation and various agencies may stipulate required standards. It is critical to adhere to these requirements, especially because many are intended to protect workers and customers.
- Trade associations and industry councils: Many industries are organized with non-government trade associations and councils. Think of bar associations in the legal profession, the Chartered Institute of Management Accountants (CIMA), or the broad International Organization for Standardization (ISO). They can help unite firms to lobby the government for preferred regulations, and to bargain together against industry-wide suppliers. They may champion best practices and stipulate rating systems, too.
- Competitors: While legal and strategic cautions must be taken when engaging with competitors, their products and services should certainly be benchmarked to ensure your offerings are competitive.

Ultimately, an organization's standards should be properly tested, approved by cross-functional leadership, and cascaded appropriately through the organization. Through training, resource allocations, and effective knowledge management, employees should be informed of and practiced in the standards for their role. Performance management systems should hold individuals and teams accountable for sustaining compliant operations. Over time, quality improvement initiatives can help teams enhance standards and elevate compliance.

Quality as Competitiveness

Our discussion of standards hinted at the next quality objective: competitiveness. In many ways, internal standards ought to reflect industry standards. To be competitive, a firm needs to deliver products and services that are comparable to market alternatives. However, comparable can also mean exceptional—better or beneficially different than competitive offerings. Compared to other products and price points in your market, customers want assurance they will get a good deal with you.

The prior section noted an excellent source for competitive intelligence: trade associations and industry councils. These groups typically provide forums for sharing best practices, distribute research on next practices, and showcase vetted vendors. They commonly clarify industry regulations and grant accreditations, certifications, licenses, and other credentials—all of which are qualifiers and indicators of quality. Many also sponsor awards and recognition programs, inviting companies to compete for advertisable designations. In many ways, these groups provide companies with an industrial measuring stick that the company can measure itself against.

Similarly, industry experts are also available in the forms of consultants. These independent experts, often with deep subject-matter expertise, offer organizations outside-in perspectives. They can be hired to share valuable knowledge and beneficial experience from other organizations. Some are skilled trainers for frontline employees or executives, while others are specialized management consultants who conduct independent analyses and help elevate standards, policies, and business strategies. Occasionally, consultants can even pretend to be customers and conduct mystery shops. Across these services, consultants can help organizations define standards, plan workways, assess performance, and improve operational excellence.

The Internet—and social media in particular—have significantly elevated the profile of another source for competitive intelligence: customers themselves. We will explore ways to learn about your own customers in the next section. For now, though, consider the invaluable insights on your competitors that can be gleaned from public ratings and reviews. Glowing comments highlight success factors that can be emulated, while complaints can showcase what *not* to do. Importantly, ratings on social media (Google, Facebook, Yelp, etc.) and on industry-specific review sites can tell future customers where you stand in the rankings.

By studying competitors and learning their lessons—across all the methods discussed in this section—your organization can elevate its offerings and position its quality in the competitive marketplace.

Quality as Customer-Centricity

While internal compliance and competitive standing are important for quality management, customer-centricity is paramount. A business cannot succeed—internally or externally—unless it ensures its customers succeed. Customer-centricity refers to delivering quality products or services that positively engage and retain customers. Retention can extend even further, with word of mouth spreading to friends and family, and even across social media to the entire marketplace. Customers—individually and at large—are the ultimate arbiters of quality.

Customers consider quality as two connected value propositions. First, customers' perceptions of the actual value of your products or services must meet or exceed their expectations.

$$\text{Customer perceived value of actual quality} \geq \text{Expected value}$$

Second, on each side of this equation, "value" is the difference between (hopefully greater) benefits and (ideally fewer) sacrifices.

$$\text{Value} = \text{Benefits}—\text{Sacrifices}$$

Table 2 outlines common benefits and sacrifices related to customer value propositions. These examples imply that the formulas above are much easier to write than materialize.

Table 2

Sample Customer Benefits and Sacrifices

Benefits	Sacrifices
- Convenience/Time-Saving	- Shopping Time
- Bargain/Cost-Saving	- Consumption Time
- Control	- Cumulative Expense
- Self-Esteem/Accomplishment	- Effort/Energy
- Status/Prestige	- Safety Risks
- Aesthetics	- Privacy Risks
- Education	- Financial Risks
- Entertainment/Enjoyment	- Psychological Risks
- Escape	- Relationship Risks
- Novelty/Newness	- Social Detriment
- Relationships	- Environmental Detriment
- Social Justice	
- Environmental Responsibility	

Note. Adapted from "Customer perceived value: A comprehensive meta-analysis," by M. Blut, D. Chaney, R. Lunardo, R. Mencarelli, and D. Grewal, 2023, *Journal of Service Research*, 0(0), Figure 1 (https://doi.org/10.1177/10946705231222295).

There are, nevertheless, frameworks that can help organizations understand their customers' value propositions and expectations for quality. Many items in Table 2 echo Abraham Maslow's hierarchy of needs (1943) and Joe Pine and James Gilmore's four realms of experiences (1998). Additionally, Parsu Parasuraman, Valarie Zeithaml, and Leonard Berry (1988) identify five key dimensions for service quality with the acronym "RATER":

- Reliability: A service (or product) performs its function accurately and consistently.
- Assurance: A business builds customers' trust through confident, knowledgeable, and courteous employees.
- Tangibles: Facilities, personnel, materials, and technology are well-maintained and visually appealing.
- Empathy: Services are personalized and reflect understanding customers' needs.
- Responsiveness: Services are prompt, and support is available and helpful.

The latter authors' popular SERVQUAL framework—a survey tool and model for assessing performance gaps—is especially recommended for evaluating service quality. Many other tools, from conjoint analyses to key driver studies, are also available to help organizations understand and address customer's needs, wants, and preferences.

Ultimately, the objective of customer-centricity is intended to ensure customers are satisfied and stay engaged with the business for future purchases. In addition to repurchasing and growing lifetime value, engagement and loyalty can also entail spreading positive word-of-mouth to entice tangential purchases by friends, families, and others in one's social network. As marketing guru Philip Kotler (2010) summarizes, "The best advertising is done by satisfied customers."

Coordinated Quality

While the three quality objectives are each important in their own right, they can coexist … or conflict. Take the value-tier carrier Spirit Airlines: they are inconsistent across flights in when it comes to charging for carry-on luggage, a service many competitors *consistently* offer complimentary and without hassle; low customer satisfaction levels reflect both the inconsistent and nickel-and-dime style of service. Conversely, competitor Southwest Airlines offers generous luggage inclusions, delivers these services consistently across flights, and takes pride in developing passenger loyalty. The latter case offers a real example of the intersection shown in Figure 1: coordinated quality arises when all three objectives of quality are simultaneously met. The firm is satisfied with internal compliance to standards, those standards allow it competitively satisfy the market, and individual customers are satisfied along the way.

Figure 1

Venn Diagram Visualizing Coordinated Quality

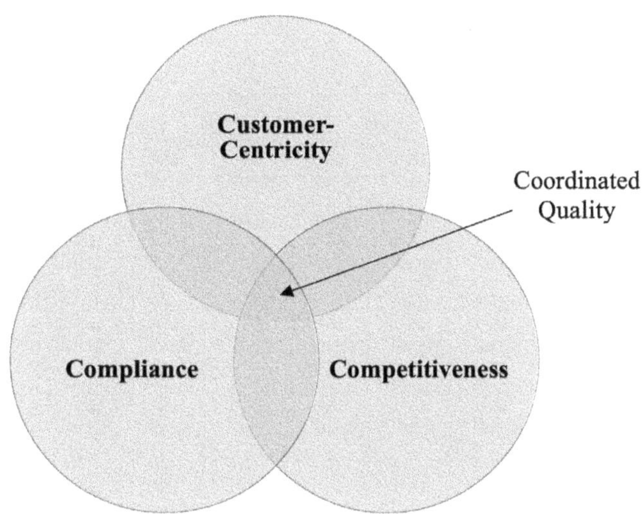

Note. Customer-centricity is intentionally atop the other objectives,
as compliance and competitiveness should support customer-centricity.

Quality Functions

It goes without saying that achieving coordinated quality—or any quality objective, for that matter—is easier said than done. Determined nevertheless, the quality management discipline offers a variety of frameworks for defining and elevating quality levels. Among the most holistic and straightforward is a four-phase sequence: plan, do, study, and act. Abbreviated as "PDSA," this model is also known as the Shewhart Cycle for its initial theorist Walter Shewhart (1939) and as the Deming Cycle for its iterator and proponent W. Edwards Deming (1982); some quality advocates also replace "study" with "check," and thus "PDSA" with "PDCA." Whichever name you prefer, the framework we are about to explore provides a structured path for quality management.

Figure 2

Shewhart/Deming Cycle for Continuous Improvement

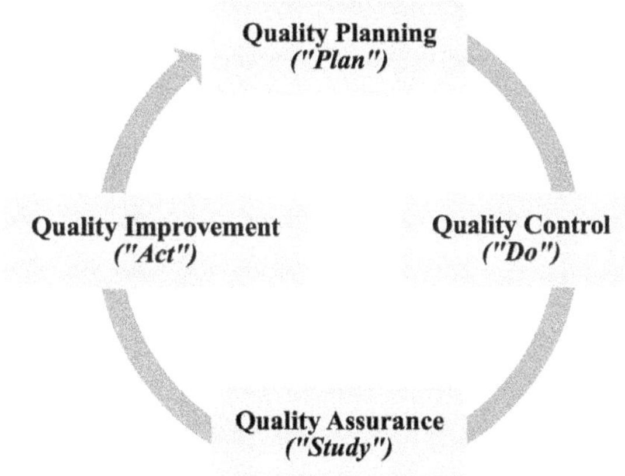

Note. Adapted from *Out of the Crisis*, by W. E. Deming, 1982, Massachusetts Institute of Technology.

Quality Planning ("Plan")

As one of the foremost gurus of quality management, Dr. Deming's philosophies permeate into PDSA: on the origins of quality, he is said to have quipped, "Every system is perfectly designed to get the results it does." Indeed, good quality can either be premeditated and planned, or it can be left to chance … and to the probability of bad quality arising. Extending this thinking, Jaguar's former CEO Dr. Ralf Speth noted, "If you think good design is expensive, you should look at the cost of bad design" (as cited in "Portraits," 2014). Quality-by-design offers a mindset for delivering compliant, competitive, and customer-satisfying products and services that reliably elevate brand equity.

Various techniques can be used to plan for *good* quality and prevent *bad* quality. Prototyping and piloting allow products and services to be tested and tweaked before full-scale production takes effect; employees from different work groups, suppliers, and even customers can be included in these tests to gather holistic perspectives from key stakeholders. Processes and policies should be documented, standardized (refer again to Table 1), and trained. Supplier evaluations and supply inspections can be used to prevent "garbage in, garbage out." Checkpoints, audits, and equipment calibrations should also be planned for downstream and ongoing evaluation. While these defect prevention measures cost time and resources, they ought to be considered investments in good quality: as Dr. Deming further noted, "The biggest cost of poor quality is when your customer buys someone else because they didn't like yours" (as cited in Lazarus, 2021).

Quality Control ("Do")

This next phase of production puts quality plans into practice. Well-trained employees and well-calibrated equipment *ideally* (we'll come back to this word) churn-out products and services, all compliant with the set standards. Check lists, punch lists, procedures, and processes should be executed with equal parts consistency, correctness, and completeness. Along the way, fool-proofing measures—called "poka-yoke"—impose warnings or barriers to mistakes. If defects do arise, they are caught and remedied before advancing further along production. What reaches the customer in the end exhibits perfect quality in every way.

Quality Assurance ("Study")

That last sentence is an admitted bluff. There are myriad reasons why defective products and services arise despite the best planning and prevent: 100% perfect quality is a virtual unicorn, and the cost to produce it is as valuable as a pot of gold at the end of a rainbow. Nevertheless, we owe it to our customers to deliver ever-better products and services, and we owe it to our employees to create quality workplaces: along the way, we can reduce costs while raising reputation. Quality assurance uncovers the steppingstones.

First, processes and their outputs should be measured along quantitative and qualitative dimensions. Sampling and inspections can be used for tangible products; inspections and mystery shops can be leveraged for services. Additional data can be gather from customer and employee feedback, whether surveyed or solicited in other ways. For quantitative factors, statistical process control (SPC) techniques can be used to assess how compliant outputs are within acceptable (or unacceptable) degrees of tolerance. Value stream analysis can be used to identify sources of waste or potential opportunities for efficiency, while critical incident technique can help trace defects and related problems. Across the board, key performance indicators (KPI) can be identified to prioritize and focus assurance efforts toward key drivers of compliance, competitiveness, and customer-centricity.

For systemic issues and opportunities, deeper analysis—called root cause analysis - is warranted to get underneath the causes and effects. Gemba walks (observation by walking around), Ohno circles (observation by standing still), and ethnographic studies (observation by watching product user or service participants) help leaders gain deeper insight. Ishikawa diagrams and the "five why's" technique help to drill into spectra of production factors: Table 3 outlines common categories for studying manufactured products versus services. Ultimately, the goals of the assurance phase are to take a pulse on the operation, and then to diagnose chronic ailments.

Table 3

Categories of Causes Effecting Quality

"Eight M's" (for Manufactured Products)	"Eight P's" (for Services)
- Manpower/Mindpower	- Product
- Machinery	- Price
- Materials	- Place
- Methods	- Promotion
- Measurements	- People
- Management	- Process
- Maintenance	- Physical Evidence
- Mother Nature (environment)	- Performance

Note. Adapted from *Reliability Engineering: A Life Cycle Approach*, by E. Bradley, 2016, CRC Press.

Quality Improvement ("Act")

Extending the medical analogy, the final phase in PDSA is all about finding sustainable remedies. An assortment of common frameworks can be applied based on the malady to be treated:

- To increase the consistency of outputs, Six Sigma offers protocols for tightening processes and driving compliance.
- To reduce waste (and operating cost), Lean helps streamline operations and eradicate non-value-adding activities.
- To elevate operational excellence, Total Quality Management (TQM) integrates all employees within a shared culture of quality.

The particular techniques of these and other frameworks are beyond the scope of this chapter, though ample resources are available online for those interested in pursuing quality.

Along those lines, quality is truly as much an outcome of good planning as it is a set of objectives to pursue. While quality improvement represents the fourth step in the PDSA cycle, the practice of continuous improvement—or "kaizen"—requires the cycle to repeat on and on. In this way, an organization's quality improves through incremental changes sustained over time.

Quality Strategy

We can apply the same PDSA cycle to develop an overarching strategy to achieve—and improve—coordinated quality. This "meta PDSA" approach begins with planning. For each quality objective, consider the goals the organization might pursue:

- Compliance might entail achieving certain passing scores on inspections, reducing defective products to below a certain target, aligning output within a limited range of acceptable tolerance, etc.
- Competitiveness could address meeting or exceeding market benchmarks, complying with industry-wide standards, ranking above peers amidst a third-party comparison, etc.
- Customer-centricity could warrant achieving certain levels of customer satisfaction scores, seeing customer complaints or problems drop below a certain amount, receiving repurchases or referrals, etc.

Measuring the organization's current baseline and scanning peers in the industry can help determine realistic targets for each goal.

To achieve the goals and objectives, activities can be designed for the traditional PDSA cycle: they can be planned, done in practice, studied for assurance, and refined for improvement. Figure 3 provides a simplified example of this approach, for a hypothetical luxury hotel. Delete the bulleted content and you can use the same matrix to strategize quality for your own organization!

Figure 3

Sample Quality Strategy Matrix Connecting for a Hotel

<table>
<tr><td colspan="2"></td><td colspan="3">Quality Objectives</td></tr>
<tr><td colspan="2"></td><td>Compliance</td><td>Competitiveness</td><td>Customer-Centricity</td></tr>
<tr>
<td rowspan="5">Quality Functions</td>
<td>Quality Goals</td>
<td>- Align with ≥ 85% of brand standards.
- Certify ≥ 95% of employees on their role-specific standards within 30 days of appointment.</td>
<td>- Earn ≥ 4-star rating by Forbes Travel Guide.
- On TripAdvisor, rank within the top 5 hotels in the market.</td>
<td>- Achieve a Net Promoter Score of ≥ 35.
- Ensure that ≥ 65% of guest complaints are resolved by the first employee with contact.</td>
</tr>
<tr>
<td>Planning</td>
<td>- Review brand standards vs. current hotel practices and earmark areas needing alignment.
- Train current team on revised standard operating processes.</td>
<td>- Visit peer hotels to identify transferable best practices.
- Compare our standards to Forbes', and plan corrections for any misalignments.</td>
<td>- Conduct a key drivers analysis to identify the most important factors affecting our guests' satisfaction.
- Plan a cadence of service trainings for all frontline and heart-of-house team members.</td>
</tr>
<tr>
<td>Control</td>
<td>- In restaurants, ensure recipe cards are correct.
- For guestrooms, appoint inspectors to verify that rooms are 100% clean and compliant before rooms are assigned to guests.</td>
<td>- Ensure reservations agents' checklists and trainings align with Forbes' standards.
- When "influencers" are detected on the arriving guest list, triple-check their rooms pre-arrival.</td>
<td>- At the front desk, install a poka-yoke alert to prevent guests from being checked into already-occupied rooms.
- For in-room dining, apply the "do not move" rule for guests assigned to rooms with amenities.</td>
</tr>
<tr>
<td>Assurance</td>
<td>- Hire a mystery shop firm to evaluate compliance with internal standards.
- Ensure the head chefs sample dishes throughout each meal period.</td>
<td>- Hire Forbes to conduct practice mystery shops.
- Monitor social media rankings for hotels in the market, and share trends and analyses with department managers.</td>
<td>- Collect, respond to, and analyze guest survey feedback.
- Monitor social media profiles for additional guest feedback, responding and analyzing accordingly.</td>
</tr>
<tr>
<td>Improvement</td>
<td>- Use audit findings to identify areas of non-compliance, and create corrective action plans.
- Create a task force to recommend process tweaks to reduce common room cleanliness defects.</td>
<td>- Use audit findings to identify areas of non-compliance, and create corrective action plans.
- Looking at the 5 closest competitors, conduct an "us vs. them" gap analysis and strategize ways to out-perform.</td>
<td>- Use critical incident technique to identify recurring problems most impacting guest satisfaction, and strategize corrections.
- Experiment with sound-proofing materials to reduce noise issues.</td>
</tr>
</table>

Conclusion

From manufacturing plants to auto mechanics to medical offices, quality counts. Compliance with internal standards can reduce cost while delivering more reliable experiences. Competitive considerations can ensure these experiences not only stack up against marketplace peers, but ultimately stand out in the eyes of customers. And on customer-centricity, quality breeds satisfaction … along with intent to return, repurchase, and refer to others. With these objectives in mind, we considered a four-phase cycle for assessing and improving the quality of experiences. Everything then integrated into a strategy for operating and achieving coordinated quality. Said another way, we defined quality approaches to customer experience management.

References

Blut, M., Chaney, D., Lunardo, R., Mencarelli, R., & Grewal, D. (2023). Customer perceived value: A comprehensive meta-analysis. *Journal of Service Research*, *0*(0). https://doi.org/10.1177/10946705231222295

Bradley, E. (2016). *Reliability Engineering: A Life Cycle Approach*. CRC Press.

Deming, W. E. (1982). *Out of the Crisis*. Massachusetts Institute of Technology.

Kotler, P., Kartajaya, H., & Setiawan, I. (2010). *Marketing 3.0: From products to customers to the human spirit*. John Wiley & Sons.

Maslow, A. H. (1943). A theory of human motivation. *Psychological Review*, 50(4), 370–396. https://doi.org/10.1037/h0054346

Lazarus, I. R. (2021). *Cost of poor quality*. Quality Magazine.

Parasuraman, A., Zeithaml, V. A., & Berry, L. L. (1988). SERVQUAL: A multiple-item scale for measuring consumer perception of service quality. *Journal of Marketing*, 64(1).

Pine, B. J., & Gilmore, J. H. (1998). Welcome to the experience economy. *Harvard Business Review*, 76(4).

Portraits. (2014). *San José State University, College of the Humanities and the Arts Expressions*, 15.

Shewhart, W. A. (1939). *Statistical Method From the Viewpoint of Quality Control*. The Graduate School, U.S. Department of Agriculture.

Recommended Readings

Denove, C., & Power, J. D. (2006). *Satisfaction: How every great company listens to the voice of the customer*. Penguin Group.

Maleyeff, J. (2021). *Service science: Analysis and improvement of business processes*. Routledge.

Maleyeff, J. (2022). *Quality service management: A guide to improving business processes*. Routledge.

Pyzdek, T., & Keller, P. (2013). *The handbook for quality management: A complete guide to operational excellence* (2nd ed.). McGraw-Hill.

Torres, E. N., & Zhang, T. (2023). *Customer service marketing: Managing the customer experience*. Routledge.

Chapter 14—Understanding the Human Element in CX

Mark Borst

"Customers are human beings with emotions, not transactions with expiration dates."
Kate Nasser

Introduction

Despite our impulse to count, measure, quantify, and transact (all of which are important to successful enterprise), client experience is a fundamentally human endeavor. This chapter will focus on human-to-human relationships as a key value driver in client experience (CX) design and organizational success. Let me illustrate with a personal story.

My wife Marilyn is an archaeologist and theologian. She forms strategic partnerships between faith-based organizations in the west and Indigenous churches in far-flung places throughout the middle east, where she frequently travels. Occasionally I accompany her. Back in 2017, we were sitting in our apartment in Beirut, Lebanon, waiting for word regarding the status of our Syrian visas. We had planned to fly to Qamishli, a city in the northeast region of Syria, near the Iraqi border. We were pessimistic about our visas because earlier in the day the U.S. had bombed a Syrian Air Force base. So, we were stunned when we got word that our visas had been granted.

We quickly boarded a chartered Jeep and headed to Damascus. At the airport, our Lebanese guide engaged in animated discussions with a succession of security officials, all of whom thwarted our efforts to gain access to our departure gate. Our guide explained that they were convinced our visas were fraudulent—why would the Syrian government issue us visas when our government had strafed their Air Force base on that very day? Eventually, we were ushered into an interior office, where we were seated at a large desk for an interview with yet another official.

As he reviewed our documents, we took a visual survey of the room. Marilyn's gaze settled upon a large, framed photograph of an auspicious gathering of Syrian clergy from a variety of faith practices. She began to call them out by their names—a pastor, a priest, an archbishop, an imam—10 in all. The Syrian official looked up at us, smiled broadly and declared, "You are friends of Syria!" He stamped our visas and sent us on our way.

Human-Centric Perspectives

What does this have to do with CX? It is quite simple: CX is fundamentally human. Just as we got our visas stamped because of our human connections, successful enterprise is highly dependent on meaningful human relationships, both inside and outside of an organization. While this may seem obvious, there are persistent factors that mitigate against it, not the least of which is the relentless pursuit of profit. Few would disagree with business guru Peter Drucker's mid-20th century assertion that "The purpose of business is to get and to keep customers." But in our 21st century economy, reaching consensus on how this might be accomplished is widely divergent. Transactional thinking is an easy default, and let's face it, it's next to impossible to quantify meaningfulness. Or is it?

In his book The Moral Molecule, neuro-economist Paul Zak presents a more nuanced point of view. "Harvard Business School's expert on the service industry Frances Frei reminds her students that that the basic idea behind business is to 'be of service.' Serving others causes the release of oxytocin[12] and begins the virtuous cycle of moral behavior. Markets give us the chance to serve others every day."[13] Zak goes on to say that "this virtuous cycle induced by trade can be diminished anytime profit replaces people as the central concern" of business.

In their seminal and still highly prescient 1999 book, The Experience Economy, authors Joseph Pine and James Gilmore define the progression of economic value over the last 120 years. In the late nineties and early aughts, we were in the throes of the Experience Economy. Pine and Gilmore astutely labeled the subsequent level of economic value as the Transformation Economy. In this economy, they assert, the customer becomes the product. In other words, a human (or organization) is somehow transformed. A customer goes into the gym fat and comes out skinny. A customer goes into the hair salon ugly and comes out beautiful. In my area of business, a customer suffering with carpal tunnel syndrome might very well eliminate their condition simply because we showed them how to properly adjust their task chair. It does not matter how much they ultimately spent on the chair (transaction); it matters how they use it (make meaning) to transform their life.

Indeed, transformational client experience is a critical driver for successful organizations today. Pine and Gilmore describe this in terms of client *aspiration:* "To what do customer aspire?" Essential to every transformation is understanding what customers truly need to become and how far away they are from fulfilling those needs within themselves, even if they do not realize it."[14] For providers of goods and services in this economic reality, the operative verb is *guide*. Does your business plan either implicitly or explicitly assert that *guiding* your customers is a value driver?

There are additional human-centric "economies" worth citing, such as the Purpose Economy, the Creative Economy, and the Maker Economy. Inherent in each of these economic values is a preoccupation with human behavior—more specifically, fundamental human impulses and values. Imagine a world of commerce in which these values formed the connection between business organizations and customers. This is a world where CX practitioners might play an essential role.

In her book, Chief Customer Officer 2.0, CX expert Jeanne Bliss suggests that "Everyone has the right thinking. Now we need to change *our behavior.* "She provides a road map for how to get there with "five competencies":

- Honor and manage clients as assets.
- Align around experience.
- Build a client listening path.
- Provide proactive experience reliability and innovation.
- Offer one company leadership, accountability, and culture.[15]

None of these steps are explicitly transactional. They *are* client-centric, purpose-driven, and highly dependent on employee engagement. Organizational purpose is propulsive when these factors align. When an organization

---

12   Oxytocin is a neurochemical known to decrease stress and increase trust.

13   Zak, Paul, The Moral Molecule, New York, Penguin, 2012, page 178

14   Pine, Joseph, and Gilmore James, The Experience Economy, Boston, Harvard Business Review Press, 1999, pp. 262–263

15   Bliss, Jeanne 2015, Chief Customer Officer 2.0, Hoboken, John Wiley & Sons, page 16.

elevates purpose, it taps in the power of making meaning, and provides context for everything it does.[16] There is an elusive aspirational quality at work here, however. For a sense of purpose to seep into all the cultural cracks and crevices, companies must instill a sense of client connectedness in their associates. They must nurture a deeply felt deferential posture acknowledging that purpose always involves something outside of ourselves. How does client-centricity take root as an authentic component of a company's marketing strategy? It starts with internal and external client relationships. It starts with human behavior.

CX Guru Bruce Temkin[17] offers further wisdom regarding organizational purpose in his 4 CX Core Competencies:

1. Leaders align the organization around a shared purpose.
2. Organizational purpose is translated into individual behaviors.
3. Employees find meaning in their roles.
4. Organizations share their purpose with clients.

Taken together, the Bliss and Temkin frames deliver a wholistic summary of an intrinsically human CX initiative. They are both committed to client listening as an act of value.[18] And we catch a glimpse into why the world of CX has spawned additional "X Disciplines" such as Experience Management (XM), and Employee Experience (EX).

Applying B2B Experience to B2C and H2H—a Journey in CX Initiatives

My experience as a CX practitioner is in the business-to-business (B2B) sector. The principles and practices discussed in this chapter are applicable in the business-to-consumer (B2C) sector as well. Meanwhile, the lexicon in the marketing community has expanded to include another sector: human-to-human (H2H). H2H is an approach to marketing that actively strips everything back to the simple reality that people buy from people. It encourages organizations to treat individuals as human beings rather than "personas" or other representations of customers/groupings. There are many ways to parse this, and I will highlight several examples throughout this chapter.

In 2013, the CFO of the company I worked for appointed me to create a CX initiative. This was a radical move for our $120 million enterprise. Our CFO had become convinced that our only differentiator was experience—NOT price, as we were committed to *not* being known as a low-cost provider. NOT quality and innovation, although we were known for both. Our only differentiator was experience. The company's headquarters were in Atlanta, with acquired offices in Birmingham, Alabama, and Nashville, Tennessee. One of my earliest tasks was to work with the leadership team to develop one company culture so that we could design and deliver a consistent client experience across the enterprise.

It is a challenge to describe my former company's industry. I would place them in the "service" sector. But we provided a very sophisticated and multi-faceted offering in the form of *goods*, such as furniture solutions,

---

16   See Hurst, Aaron, The Purpose Economy, Boise, Elevate, 2014

17   See Qualtrics XM Institute Insight Report (Bruce Temkin), The Four Customer Experience Core Competencies, 2019

18   Bliss, Jeanne 2015, Chief Customer Officer 2.0, Hoboken, John Wiley & Sons, pp.111–136

interior architecture products, and *services*, such as evidence-based design solutions, asset management, move management, and technology interfaces for corporate, healthcare, and education facilities. Projects ranged in size from a single task chair to multiple 20,000 square foot office tower floorplates. We designed and furnished spaces for innovative classroom buildings and innovative healthcare facilities. The sales team worked closely with influencers in corporate real estate and interior architecture. It was a complex business. In an early journey mapping exercise, we identified fifty-three steps in a single client "transaction."

Fostering a Client-Centric Culture

Until now in this writing, I have been using the words "client" and "customer" interchangeably. Early on in our CX initiative, we elected to refer to our customers as clients. Though this may seem like a small step, it had a transformational impact on the organization. Not only did it bring a sense of agency to our client interactions, it also significantly improved our organizational professionalism. Furthermore, we used the same nomenclature within the company, referring to "internal clients" anytime one associate acted in service to another. One of the descriptors we included in our journey mapping process was "Who is the client of this step?" Often, it was an internal associate.

To further inculcate CX into our organizational DNA, we convened the "Client Council," which was comprised of 21 associates from all three locations. It included employee representatives from every department: front-line employees and executives alike. Included (by design) were installers, designers, VPs, middle managers, sales associates, and others. The Client Council meets once a month for an entire day to create and hone client journey maps, and to uncover touchpoints that needed improvement. We defined touchpoints as "every interaction—physical, communication, human, and sensory, WITH and WITHIN the organization." This definition, as well as the concept for the Client Council was provided to us by CX expert Hank Brigman, author of "Touchpoint Power,"[19] who served as my coach and consultant at the outset of our CX program.

After the Client Council identified touchpoints needing improvement, we launched inter-departmental Discovery Workshops spearheaded by the associates whose teams were responsible for that touchpoint. This was a comprehensive, employee-centric undertaking. Employees travelled from Atlanta and Nashville to our Birmingham office, a 1.5-hour trip. This commitment necessitated a day away from the office or the field, but it reaped palpable benefits. People felt valued by the organization. Leaders emerged. Company practices improved and processes became more streamlined. And the client experience became a singular focus across the entire organization.

The Discovery Workshops had titles like "What's in Your Toolbox?" and, "It Takes HOW Long?" I collaborated closely with the Vice President of HR to ensure that CX and employee engagement were fully integrated. We designed workshops around client empathy, process improvement, and client conversations based on the journey mapping output produced by the Client Council. We trained frontline installers and service techs to actively listen to clients, especially when they were on the job site. Often a work area was directly adjacent to client's active workspaces. What conversations did they overhear? What impressions were they sharing? Did you gain insight into how our clients think?

---

19   Brigman, Hank. Atlantic Beach, William Henry Publishing, 2013, page xix, page 174

Many of our techs made this a priority, and they eagerly shared stories at team meetings and workshops, or over a cup of coffee with me in the field. This qualitative feedback channel eventually eclipsed our NPS Survey results, which, despite our best efforts, tended to yield unhelpful quantitative feedback. We also empowered administrative associates to suggest process improvements and innovative ideas for additional Discovery Workshops.

The artifacts of the Client Council and the Touchpoint Workshops—comprised of a couple of hundred feet of butcher paper with journey maps, process maps, and empirical data—were on prominent display throughout our offices, which functioned as work laboratories for visiting clients. Not only were we entirely transparent about our processes with our clients, but the output on display was also a powerful visual reminder of daily team accomplishments. Clients showed a great deal of interest in these maps. We began to co-create journey maps with clients, often at their facilities and engaging with their teams. This process yielded multiple benefits. Clients provided insights into their processes, resulting in a journey design that blended client processes, needs, and aspirations with our processes. In the current era of hybrid work settings, a well-facilitated online journey mapping experience will have the same outcome. There are a host of online mapping tools available, many of which provide delightful user interface experiences.

Client Journey STAGES.

Align around experience. **CLIENT EXPERIENCE** *is the* **operational** *answer to these questions.*

Relationship (develop)	Business Issues	Research	Selection	Installation	Usage	Relationship (nurture)
What reason do I have to engage with them?	Did they make me smarter about my choices?	How will they help me? Can I trust them?	Will they help me select the right solution?	Did they install per my needs and on time? Did they get it right the first time?	Is the solution delivering? Do they show up when things go wrong?	Do they know me and help me proactively?

Evolution of Client Journey Mapping—From Steps to Stages

Eventually we adopted, with a nod to Jeanne Bliss, a broader view of the client journey. We began to focus on journey *stages* rather than journey *steps*. To be sure, the steps were still important, but we gave them a fresh context within the stages of the journey as illustrated in the graphic above. This perspective helped us better understand the client journey across potential silos, and it recalibrated our understanding of the arc of the client journey. It begins with developing a client relationship and culminates in nurturing that relationship. At each stage, we engage key client questions, to which client experience is the operational answer.[20]

---

20   Bliss, Jeanne 2015, Chief Customer Officer 2.0, Hoboken, John Wiley & Sons, page 101

The questions form an impetus for further journey mapping, now created within each stage. This has the potential for providing granular, accessible detail in an extraordinarily complex business model. Here, we took particular care to avoid siloed thinking, because the client journey still occurred across these seven stages, which brings up another point.

In my industry, these stages encompassed an 18-month decision-making process. If the team were unsuccessful at engaging at the initial relationship stage, chances are they would not be invited to the party until the selection stage, which is where the transaction typically takes place. If at this stage the client's focus is on lowest cost, it is too late to develop a meaningful relationship with them. When price becomes the only differentiator, the prospect of powerful human connections diminishes. As I stated at the outset, and it bears repeating, successful CX is predicated on human relationships as a primary value driver. The duration and depth of relationships matter.

At my company, we twisted ourselves into pretzels trying to avoid using the word sales or salesperson. We used job titles such as Workplace Consultant, Client Success Manager, and Client Development Specialist. These were all reasonable titles, I think, but doubly challenging because many of our salespeople were paid 100% commission. Most major client decisions are made at the C-suite level, and it is no easy task to gain an audience, much less engage in meaningful conversation about business issues that go far deeper than the price or design of a widget. Recognizing opportunities to "make meaning" for clients is not likely to happen when a seller is fretting about how many widget sales it takes to put their kid through college. Still, when a client is spending seven figures to revamp their workspace, they have every right to ask challenging questions: What reason do I have to engage? Will they make me smarter about my choices? How will they help me with my choices? Can I trust them? Again, Bliss offers superlative advice—client experience is the operational answer to these questions.

Educating Through Dialogue—the Power of Client Conversations

Even as we continued to battle the relentless undertow of transactional thinking, I was resolutely committed to consultative storytelling as a client experience strategy. I designed a tool to stem the tide, a workshop entitled, "Client Conversations." One of the first questions we posited was, "Is it getting harder to be heard by your clients?" The workshop was a content-rich educational experience that traced the history of work and the workplace from 1900 to 2018. It layered technological innovation with changes in the workplace. I juxtaposed workplace design research from 1968 and 2018. I pulled multiple quotes from each body of research and asked the participants to guess when they were written. They answered incorrectly 50% of the time. What was the common denominator of research conducted 50 years apart? Human-factored design.

A subsequent discussion pointed out how these human factors serve as business drivers. We might be surprised to learn that creativity, well-being, technology interface (User Experience), biophilia, access and privacy, and diversity were formational influences in 1968, when Robert Probst invented the first panel system, also known as office landscape, which ultimately devolved into cubicles and cubicle farms in the 1980s. And these factors were formational influencers in 2018 as well, when hybrid workplaces and work-from-home strategies had begun to proliferate in pre-pandemic corporate America.

As is often true in business-to-business commerce, clients often don't know what they don't know about your offering. A conversation about how to support well-being in the workplace trumps a conversation about the cost of a cubicle any day of the week. Because of client conversation training, our frontline client consultants were better able to contextualize work and workplace issues, and consequently go deeper with skeptical C-level clients to "make meaning." Though this is an industry-specific example, there are additional aspects of this initiative which are agnostic to industry sectors. After all, we're advocating for client conversations, and no two clients are alike. And conversations are human to human.

Mastering the Art of Inquiry—Enhancing Client Experience Through Strategic Questioning

Another aspect of the conversational character of client experience is the art of inquiry. As mentioned previously, many B2B clients may not comprehend the vast array of potential solutions available to help solve a business problem, even a problem they don't know they have. Asking the right questions of your clients is a baseline for uncovering fresh thinking, and for developing trust. Implicit in our client journey mapping process was an assumption that there might be a better way. We framed our approach to client problem-solving utilizing the ADKAR method, which is based on the idea that organizational change can only happen when individuals change.[21] And, we actively engaged design-thinking methodologies, which do not assume one right answer to a challenge. Rather, design thinking *iterates* toward a *better* answer. An effective opening client question might be, "Where is your pressure coming from?" We used various aspects of these frames to design the client experience at every stage in their journey with our company. In fact, we developed discovery workshops to hone our associates' questioning skills, which became an offering I provided to clients via interactive Zoom workshops during the pandemic.

Yet another compelling iteration of this concept comes from the late Harvard Business Professor Clayton Christensen in his book, Competing Against Luck. Christensen offers remarkably simple but powerful insights in his Jobs Theory approach to the client. Christensen asserts that "clients don't *buy* products or services: they *pull* them into their lives to make progress."[22] Wait, what? Do clients have lives? Indeed, they do, and we once again return to the human aspect of client experience. He expands the metaphor further. The progress the client is trying to make is the "job" they are trying to get done, and the client "hires" your offering to solve these jobs. Our clients hired an ergonomic task chair to eliminate carpal tunnel for their associates. They "hired" our market research to better understand how they might use their facility as a strategic tool. Just as you might hire a Reuben sandwich to satisfy your hunger pangs.

Christensen's "jobs theory" completely validated our initial assumption that experience was our only differentiator. The jobs theory approach eliminates the transaction as the central feature of a client relationship and replaces it with a journey. Do you see where we are? Back to being guides to our clients in the Transformation Economy. And it provides yet another dimension for the way a client experiences their journey with an organization (italics mine):

UNCOVERING THE JOB

A job is the progress *an individual* seeks in each circumstance.

CREATING THE *DESIRED EXPERIENCES*

The *experiences we enable* in each of these three dimensions to *fulfill the job.*

INTEGRATING AROUND THE JOB

Aligning our internal processes with the job to *provide* the *desired experiences.*[23]

---

21   ADKAR is an acronym for Awareness, Knowledge, Ability, and Reinforcement. Jeff Hiatt, founder of Prosci

22   Christensen, Clayton, et.al, Competing Against Luck, Harper Collins, 2016, page 27.

23   IBID, page 129

Fostering Trust and Human Connection—The Heart of Client Experience

Perhaps the most crucial characteristic of the client experience in these examples is the establishment of trust. In his book, Trust Factor, Paul Zak brilliantly explores the neuroscience of trust in client relationships. As previously cited, oxytocin is the key hormonal ingredient here. "Trust begets oxytocin, which begets trustworthiness in return. Think of oxytocin as the biological basis for the Golden Rule. If you treat me nice, my brain makes oxytocin, signaling that you are a person I want to be around, so I treat you nice in return."[24]

Amongst other traits, oxytocin generates trust, empathy, and calm, focused attention. It's the "tend and befriend" neurochemical, and it's responsible for transporting narrative—storytelling. According to story-telling expert, Bernadette Jiwa, "Every one of us is in the business of changing minds. All stories—those we tell and those we believe in—are powerful catalysts for change. Stories are the cornerstone for human connection and collaboration, drivers of our thoughts and actions."[25] The telling and *believing* of stories, then, is fundamental to our humanity and it is fundamental to success with our clients. Stories are at the very core of human relationships. And it is how we learn to trust and gain the perception of being trustworthy.

Hopefully by now it is clear that the unifying thread of human-centric client experience is an unflagging preoccupation with the lives of clients. This is the quintessential value driver for successful organizations: a purpose-driven commitment to internal and external client relationships, prioritizing people over process, and cultivating an acute awareness of client "wants needs and expectations," as we did in our journey mapping, empathy mapping and onsite listening practices. Though not transactionally measurable, it is reasonable to connect outcomes to client behavior. How organizations cultivate and curate these relationships are key. Meaningful client conversations yield an increase in the depth and intimacy of the client relationship, and thus potentially the duration.[26] Client retention portends an increase in business.

To be sure, new technologies will offer new ways to measure things. Even as traditional tools such as NPS wax and wane, the potential for artificial intelligence to transform CX is still in its early stage, but on the sharp edge of what's next. Curiously, AI is already at work in human emotion, with capabilities such as hyper-personalization, predictive (behavior) analytics, and sentiment analysis. Humans are still "pushing the buttons" behind the scenes, of course, and regardless of how sophisticated AI becomes at streamlining our world, human relationships will remain at the core of B2B commerce.

The emerging disciplines of neuroeconomics, behavioral economics, and the science of transformation will continue to shape innovation in client experience strategy. What are the forces compelling or preventing change in your organization? Where do employee and client experience intersect? How is your organization transforming the lives of your clients? Are you cultivating trust? How might you borrow from a projected future (strategic foresight) to inform innovation now? How might design thinking inform a fresh approach to client relationships? A failed prototype, whether it be a product or an idea, is a sure-fire method for creating something better. What risks are you willing to take to truly innovate your offering and the client experience you craft around it? Why would a client pay for your service, other than to make their lives better? This is your organization's transcendent purpose.

---

24   Zak, Paul, Trust Factor, New York, American Management Association, 2017, page 16

25   Jiwa, Bernadette, The Right Story, Perceptive Press, 2019, page 73

26   See Reise, Andrew, How to Deliver CX Strategies That Result in Business Impact, Overland Park, andrewreise.com

Chapter 15—The Power of Employee Experience

Rich Dorfman

> *"Employees who believe that management is concerned about them as a whole per-son—not just an employee—are more productive, more satisfied, and more fulfilled. Satisfied employees mean satisfied customers, which leads to profitability."*
> **Anne M. Mulcahy, Former chairperson and CEO of Xerox Corporation**

Fueling Success Through Enrichment, Engagement, and Empowerment

Even novice CX practitioners have heard some version of the following statement… "the customer experience can be no greater than the employee experience." But in practice, does this mantra hold true? You bet it does! In today's dynamic business landscape, where competition is fierce and customer expectations are constantly evolving, companies are realizing the vital role that their employees play in driving success. Employee experience (EX) has emerged as a crucial aspect of organizational strategy, focusing on creating an enriching work environment where employees feel valued, engaged, and empowered to deliver their best. This chapter explores the significance of EX, highlighting how companies are listening to their employees, motivating them, and acting on their ideas and suggestions to drive exceptional customer experiences that fuel their sustained loyalty, and improved bottom-line performance and a competitive edge in the marketplace.

The Challenges and the Benefits of Great EX

The struggle for companies to deliver against constantly increasing employees' expectations and to leverage the full potential of their work contributions to sustain growth is greater than ever. The massive disruption caused by the pandemic diminished, for many, the important comradery felt by collaborating in-person and on premises when work shifted to a fully or mostly remote environment. Insights gleaned from surveys taken across industries during and post-Covid revealed significant numbers of employees feeling a sense of loneliness, dislocation, even exhaustion when online "work hours" crept into boundaries viewed as personal time. Even though less commuting for remote employees fostered a sense of improved work-life balance, studies also surfaced the negative consequences (for some) of reduced worker productivity and accessibility to helpful guidance stemming from insufficient direct supervision.

Manager and colleague interactions have also become less personal but more frequent via an endless array of daily virtual meetings introducing a new corporate phenomenon known as "Zoom Fatigue." This dynamic continues to strain attempts at maintaining a healthy corporate culture, especially given the fact that so many transitioned to new jobs or opted for retirement. The impact too of technology is pervasive and accelerating. AI, particularly the hype around GenAI, and other tech-enhanced productivity tools contribute to employees' sense of vulnerability and job insecurity.

Despite these and other challenges in establishing the promise of an employee-focused culture, the benefits of doing so are many. Just as customer loyalty is the precursor to long term company profits, employee loyalty directly and profoundly influences customers' opinions of the brand. When colleagues are happy, respected, motivated, and supported, they are significantly more productive, tend to stay longer, are more willing to contribute valuable insights, and engender a positive working environment. Employees thus collectively serve as "front line" brand ambassadors responsible for holding to account the promises made by Marketing.

This interconnectedness of employee satisfaction, culture, customer advocacy, and organizational health is a prime example of systems thinking and the construct illuminated in the Service Profit Chain. For a deeper understanding of this principle and core component of the CX discipline, read (re-read) Karl Sharicz' relevant chapter in his earlier book, *CX-PRO: A Practical Guide for the New Customer Experience Manager*.

The remainder of this chapter will explore several practical methods of engaging and motivating employees within an organization, along with easy-to-implement effective use cases that validate the symbiosis between EX and CX.

Leveraging the Roles of, Partnership Between CX & HR Teams

A logical corporate ally for CX practitioners to enlist in enhancing colleague experience is their HR counterparts. Both teams share the same basic goals, albeit focused on different stakeholders. Human Resources professionals prioritize employee well-being and satisfaction, their engagement and empowerment, and their rewards and recognition. CX teams are obsessed with delighting customers by helping to ensure every interaction of theirs with the brand is easy, helpful, and satisfying. Aligning the interests of both employees and customers through a thoughtful, strategic partnership of CX and HR teams is imperative for sustained business success.

Like any cross-functional collaboration, it takes effort, time, and patience to build the necessary mutual trust to achieved shared goals. For example, HR teams feel that it is their domain to manage the yearly all-employee benchmark engagement survey to assess colleagues' attitudes on a multitude of criteria and KPIs relative to peer organizations to uncover and act on identified areas for improvement. But, as a single point-in-time, standardized questionnaire initiatives, insight gaps for specific employee journeys, activities, and segments will undoubtedly be discovered. That's where the CX team can and should enter the picture in helping to address those gaps. The team would meet with the various HR leaders responsible for talent acquisition, learning & development, benefits & payroll, rewards & compensation, DEI, etc., to discuss their goals and objectives throughout the year, learning where and how employee feedback would guide their decision making. The CX practitioner thus becomes positioned, and valued, as an "insight partner" to HR by leveraging their skills in bringing actionable, invaluable voice of the employee perspectives to sustain the hard fought positive corporate culture.

Case Study: How CX and HR Teamed Up to Enhance Benefits Servicing

Consider how one CX team collaborated with their HR Benefits counterparts of a growing software company to assess and address employee feedback about a recently introduced health plan from a brand-new national provider. The Benefits team did extensive due diligence in selecting the health plan based on needs for 1) expanded network coverage (more colleagues working remotely in different states), 2) ensuring like services from the previous plan, 3) keeping rising premiums under control, and 4) checking references for quality of service. They also led multiple online educational onboarding sessions, distributed comprehensive plan FAQs and resource guides, and held office hours for one-to-one consults to ensure employees fully understood the plan and use it to manage healthcare needs.

The CX team was brought in to capture employee feedback via a survey on two dimensions of the plan rollout: 1) to assess the quality of educational efforts and ease of enrollment and 2) to learn about initial experiences using the plan and gauge the quality of the plan's member service department. Important insights were uncovered. In terms of educational onboarding, many employees wanted more specific health plan information and presented in a way that was easier to absorb, which led Benefits to create video vignettes of different scenarios placed on the company intranet. Regarding member servicing feedback, significant numbers felt that health plan agents, while nice and friendly, lacked sufficient skills in the plans and knowledge to address issues employees were experiencing. This curated insight from the CX-HR partnership was shared with the health plan's management, which resulted in the software company switching to the health plan's highest-level and most experienced agent support teams that dramatically reduced service dissatisfaction. Employee benefits, especially healthcare considering its relative cost and emotional impact, are significant drivers of overall job satisfaction. The fact that employees palpably felt the health plan's service improvement thanks to the feedback heard, understood, and acted on by HR and CX teams, satisfaction, along with retention and worker productivity increased, which continued to have an outsized impact on customer loyalty to the brand.

The Executive Welcome, Employee Roundtables & Leader-Led Listening Sessions

It's always important for employees to feel heard and appreciated to sustain a positive corporate culture. It's especially meaningful when top-of-the-house leadership is doing the active listening to demonstrate that this is expected behaviors from all managers in the organization.

Enlightened CEOs recognize this key dynamic. Many take the time to personally welcome new employees in small group sessions to share the company's history, vision, and competitive edge in the marketplace. But the most essential part of this executive "welcome to the company" best practice is in listening and responding authentically to the questions asked of new hires. This open exchange, established right from the start of the employee's journey, establishes from day one that the company values their candid feedback and contributions demonstrating a shared sense of common purpose.

Ongoing executive employee roundtables affirm this commitment beyond the glow of that initial warm welcome. Consider the powerful message sent to rank-and-file colleagues when the president or top member of senior management routinely holds unstructured meetings, either in person or virtually, with folks from a rotating set of departments to hear their concerns, dialogue on their suggestions for improvement, and simply enable direct, unencumbered access to the "big brass" without their direct supervisors present to encourage candor. A member of the CX team should be a regular, silent attendee of these conversations to listen to the feedback, take notes of next steps and proposed action items, and then share a curated, unattributed summary to the employees' division head to follow through on. And that's the secret sauce—making sure the employees feel heard that their suggestions were put into play where possible to improve efficiency and often make a positive difference in their work lives. By logical extension, a streamlined internal workflow and elimination of employee pain points routinely leads to improved customer satisfaction when the tasks they seek to accomplish with the company also get easier.

Case Study: Leveraging Employee Feedback to Customize & Streamline Call Center Operations

The division head of a bank's contact center holds monthly virtual meetings with its mostly remote (since Covid) agents so she could hear directly from them how things are going. Over several months and innumerable sessions, consistent feedback surfaced about the rising tide of fraud calls coming into the contact center.

Customers were increasingly becoming victims of identity theft, scammers, and fraudulent purchases causing them to feel anxious and frustrated. This dynamic elevated the stress among agents as well given how emotional these calls were and how long they took, which dramatically impacted average handling and wait times in the entire department, further exacerbating customer tensions.

The division head wanted to better understand what agents had to go through to effectively manage these calls, including the systems needed, processes employed, departments involved, and communications sent to customers that impacted final resolution. She called in the help of the CX team for a deep dive. The CX team collaborated closely with contact center leaders to jointly develop a discussion guide and then lead a series of focus groups with agents to uncover the full scope and scale of activities, especially the most impactful pain points, in managing these complex fraud calls. Key insights poured out of these facilitated conversations leading to many process improvements along the way.

The most dynamic and impactful one involved the creation of a specialty team that became known as The Fraud Squad. This group of seasoned agents, which had the benefit of a higher job grade and commensurate salary, became the front-line specialists overseeing fraud. A unique fraud option was created in the Interactive Voice Response (IVR) queue to immediately direct callers to this team and all generalist agents were directed to warm transfer any customers mentioning fraudulent activity challenges to The Fraud Squad. The impact was profound and immediate. Average call handle and wait times dipped significantly as non-fraud calls were much shorter in duration. Plus, customer call satisfaction quickly reached the highest levels ever recorded in the contact center given the proper dispositioning of calls to the agents best equipped to handle them. A true win-win was realized thanks to effective listening, then appropriately acting on colleague feedback.

Making It Fun & Empowering: Innovating Employee Experience

There are many tried and true techniques beyond those already referenced to ensure employees are made to feel as valued contributors to the organization's success. Corporate recognition programs, for example, are a staple at most firms in institutionalizing the thanking, recognizing, and rewarding colleagues for jobs well done and accomplishments that went beyond normal duties. Simple gestures too, like managers taking their staff out to lunch or the whole department getting together for a fun and games break from the routine on occasion are sure-fire morale boosters. Mix in a group volunteer project or two throughout the year and the culture of caring extends beyond the team to the community at large, bringing a sense of togetherness that's worth more than a paycheck in many cases.

But when activities can effectively combine ongoing impactful process improvement, felt by both employees and customers with a sense of work enrichment and empowerment by colleagues, magic happens. Take the innovative approach below as a case in point.

Case Study: The Power of Crowdsourcing Issues & Collaborating to Fix Them

The manager of the operations department of a wholesale electrical supply company used to have a physical suggestion box outside her office to collect and act on colleagues' ideas for improvement. Some ideas were insightful resulting in positive changes. Some were vague or unhelpful. Most were anonymous. She knew there had to be a more effective and efficient way to get quality suggestions into the idea funnel while creating enhanced engagement among her ops staff in figuring viable solutions for them. So, she reached out to her CX insights partners for guidance.

The CX team partnered with their digital strategy counterparts to identify and onboard a SaaS platform solution specifically designed for internal stakeholders to collaborate on idea crowdsourcing to identify viable candidates for implementation. The respective teams recognized from the outset that a tool specifically designed to foster collaboration among teams to source, synthesize, and systematically action on improvement suggestions would be a boon to enterprise innovation, not to mention reinforce the spirit of cooperation towards a common mandate and enculturate teamwork.

The CX team gathered the leaders within the department to introduce the concept and walk them through the mechanics of how ideas would flow through the funnel. Every team member in the group was granted access to the platform, which they decided to call Sprout (as in "begin to grow" or "shoot forth") and encouraged to use this "online idea lab" as a replacement for the old-fashioned, analog suggestion box. While the technology proved easy-to-use for colleagues yet sophisticated enough to enable the administrator to productively manage and communicate the idea pipeline, the beauty of Sprout lay in its organizational brilliance as noted in the following three critical success factors:

1. **Tying ideas to an individual**. This dynamic caused the submitter to be more thoughtful around quality suggestions and not being able to hide behind anonymity as peers and managers would have full transparency. The other main benefit was the recognition afforded the employee by the team when their idea made it all the way to implementation, thus making her proud while motivating others to offer up their own ideas.

2. **Gamifying the process to make it fun and empowering**. Submitters would creatively name their idea, then choose or create a visual to represent it. They would also be required to suggest how the idea would benefit team members and or the customers, so the suggestion had an impactful benefit behind it. Once the idea was placed "on the wall," colleagues would add their comments using @ mentions of team members to promote engagement and vote on the ideas they liked best to move them up the ladder for higher consideration on remediation efforts. Awards were even given out to the most creative idea or the individual who had the greatest number of ideas contributed within a given month to further enrich the experience.

3. **Forming subcommittees to ensure Sprout stayed fresh and productive.** One subcommittee was tasked as "cheerleaders" called Moderators to communicate Sprout's wins and to encourage ongoing colleague engagement for their ideas submitted, comments added, or votes registered. Moderators also led the celebrations when ideas made it all the way through the vetting process to implementation. To get the suggestions to the finish line, the Idea Explorer subcommittee, comprised of seasoned, operationally savvy managers in the department, would meet weekly to discuss newly submitted ideas and report back on the progress being made across the organization that often-involved collaboration outside of operations on the suggestions deemed worthy of pursuit and practical to engineer.

The results of the Sprout crowdsourcing initiative, measured both in numbers of pain points identified and fixed in the department and in the comradery and teamwork engendered, continue to pay dividends more than one year after launch. The program has been so successful, the contagiously positive impact has inspired other departments within the company to embrace the program not wanting to be left out of the fun and the productivity gains to crow about.

Conclusion

In conclusion, the employee experience stands as the bedrock of customer loyalty, serving as the bridge between promises made and promises kept. The satisfaction, motivation, and empowerment of employees form the essential prerequisites behind the enduring allegiance of customers. As the frontline ambassadors of a brand, employees hold the key to delivering on the pledges made to customers. Actively listening to their ideas, validating their input, and acknowledging the vital role of their talent and experience are imperative steps toward fostering a culture of mutual respect and continuous improvement. By prioritizing the well-being and engagement of employees, organizations not only enhance the quality of their internal operations but also elevate the seamless experience customers have with their brand. Ultimately, investing in the employee experience is not merely a matter of good practice but a strategic imperative for companies aiming to thrive in today's competitive landscape. It is through the empowerment and appreciation of employees that businesses can authentically fulfill their commitments to customers, ensuring enduring loyalty and sustainable success.

Chapter 16—Customer Experience Career Paths: How to Find a Job in Customer Experience

Laurie Gray

> *"The only way to do great work is to love what you do. If you haven't found it yet, keep looking. Don't settle."*
>
> **Steve Jobs**

If you are an experienced employee or if you are new to the world of work, your goal in landing a position is to successfully identify and join an organization that understands the value of customer experience, while also identifying you as a candidate to move their organization forward. Ideally this will be a position that provides you with support as you grow and allows you to focus on areas that are of greatest interest to you. Regardless of the amount of competition for roles when you are searching, approaching the job search process with a plan sets you up for success. After reading this chapter, you'll understand how to approach your job search process, and be confident as you begin a rewarding career.

The Job Search Plan

The goal of a job search is to present yourself as the best candidate for a role and earn the position. You'll need to prove your experience and forecast and communicate your value to justify your salary. At the same time, the interview process is an opportunity for you to determine if the company will be a fit for you. How will you present yourself as the best candidate? One of my strongest recommendations is to consider yourself a product and market yourself as a product marketer would, with the intention of driving curiosity and excitement to earn interviews and eventually one or more job offers. To complete this successfully, you'll need to understand how job searches work and follow the best practices that honor potential employers—your customers.

I had the opportunity to speak with Allison Herbert, a digital product experience colleague, to gain her perspective on product marketing best practices as they relate to positioning yourself during your search. Her advice—embrace and actively address the four fundamental tasks that are key to successful product marketing. She suggested these four elements as described in a book by Martina Lauchengco titled "Loved." To accomplish this successfully, you will need to dedicate time and attention to performing each of the roles simultaneously to help successfully promote yourself as the right candidate for the job.

1. Ambassador—connecting with people and building your network.
2. Strategist—focusing on specific roles and organizations.
3. Storyteller—sharing the right information to intrigue and engage potential employers.
4. Evangelist—actively engaging in self-advocacy and self-promotion.

Operating as an Ambassador

Job-seeker ambassadors focus on building relationships through networking, which can be defined as a continuous process of discovering and building relationships with others. These relationships can be with professionals in the same or different fields, friends, relatives, or neighbors. Some of the people in my network are other parents I've met through my children's extracurricular activities. You can also build your network through professional organizations such as local or national CXPA chapters.

Networking can offer many benefits during a job search.

- Although the specific percentage estimates vary by source and over time, there is general agreement that many job openings are never advertised publicly. Networking allows you to learn about these unadvertised opportunities from your connections.
- People within your network can provide valuable insights into companies, roles, and industries, helping you plan your job search and prepare for interviews.
- Employers may prefer to hire candidates who are recommended by someone they know and trust within their network. A referral from someone within your network may increase your chances of getting hired and may shorten the hiring process since you've been pre-vetted.
- Engaging with your network can help you to learn from more experienced professionals, gain mentorship, and stay updated on industry trends and best practices, ultimately making you more marketable.
- A strong network can boost your confidence during the job search process and provide emotional support from others who have been through similar experiences.

Your LinkedIn profile is a powerful vehicle when it comes to networking. It allows you to connect with former colleagues, classmates, and others in your field. You can join affinity groups, follow companies and influencers, and stay up to date on industry trends and news, making you able to have an informed opinion to share with prospective employers. Although the algorithm continues to change, creating posts, responding to others' posts, and creating and publishing your own original content on the platform can all increase your visibility.

Networking can also improve your visibility to potential employers, help you obtain visibility toward positions, and help you gain access to people who work for companies where there are positions available. People understand the benefit of connecting directly with recruiters and hiring managers but are often confused on how to connect and network with them. One of the questions I'm asked frequently is how to network. I typically break down networking into three categories, affinity networking, organizational networking, and strategic job networking.

- Engage in **affinity networking** by connecting with professionals in your field of interest. Send brief, sincere messages expressing your shared interest and desire to connect. Utilize online meetings and events to share your profile link or display your LinkedIn QR code at in-person events to connect with others.
- For **organizational networking**, connect with individuals from meaningful organizations, whether current or prospective employers, or influential nonprofits. Reach out with concise, genuine messages expressing your interest in learning more about their organization. Follow their company profiles on LinkedIn for insights and additional opportunities to connect.
- In **strategic job networking**, connect with individuals who can aid your job search, such as employees or contacts of your target companies, or influencers, thought leaders and others in your community who are well connected. There is a lot of benefit in connecting with people in these pivotal roles; they may be able to facilitate connections to others in your target organizations. Finally, when

considering strategic job networking, aim to connect directly with hiring managers or recruiters when possible.

Regardless of the type of connection you're seeking to make, written requests to connect should always be brief, clear on the request, grammatically correct, and respectful. I have found the following message formats to be successful. Of course, you can and should modify any of these examples to suit your specific situation, and there are more versions of these messages, but this should get you started. It is also a courtesy to thank your new connection if they respond favorably and begin a conversation if appropriate.

- Affinity networking request example for someone with whom you share many connections:
  - *"Hello, (name), I see we share many connections, but we aren't connected yet. I'd like to connect. Thank you."*
- Organizational request example:
  - *"Hello, (name), I see you work for (company name). I'm interested in learning more about the organization and would like to connect. Thank you."*
  - This often works best if you're in a similar area of operation e.g., connecting with someone in a Customer Experience or related role.
- Strategic, job oriented, second-degree connection request:
  - *"Hello, (name). I am currently seeking my next role and I'm interested in (organization name). I see you are connected to (second degree connection's name) at that company and I'm wondering if you'd consider introducing me to them. Thank you."*

A relationship with a recruiter during your job hunt may also be a great idea. According to Madison Jinks, a Customer Experience and User Experience recruiter at Synergis, a good recruiter can greatly enhance your search. They can function as your advocate and provide valuable support throughout the process. Look for an ethical recruiter who prioritizes your interests, but remember, it's a partnership, so stay engaged with them. Collaborating with a recruiter doesn't mean handing off your job search entirely; you'll still need to take an active role in directing your own search efforts.

Operating as a Strategist

When you're acting as a job-seeking strategist, your focus should be on translating your career goals into actionable plans. When you're operating as a strategist, you'll be focusing on the following key tasks.

- **Setting your near- and longer-term career goals**. Consider setting near and long-term goals, informed by what you learn during your Ambassador activities. A quick way to frame your near-term career goals is based on an exercise suggested by my career coach, Jerry Seufert. He advised me to make a list of those things that matter most in and out of work and prioritize them. Once you perform this activity, you can then use this information to form career goals.
- **Conducting analysis to identify and plan for current and emerging trends as well as potential roadblocks you're likely to encounter**. As you begin, consider the job market's temperature and financial climate—is it an employer's market or a job seeker's? Organizations adjust hiring based on financial results and market trends, and this will affect your approach and resources for landing a role. Large-scale trends like AI significantly impact business operations and subsequent plans for hiring; your best bet will be to stay informed and leverage these trends to your advantage. Highlight

your expertise in emerging areas through thought leadership or portfolio elements to appeal to potential employers.

- **Determining what resources you can allocate to your search**. Assess how much time you can dedicate to career ambassadorship, strategy, storytelling, and evangelizing. If you're unemployed, you may be able to treat your search as a full-time endeavor; if you're employed, you'll need to balance time accordingly. If financial resources are a concern, there are many affordable ways to develop skills through options such as free or low-cost classes by major tech organizations or local groups. If you can, investing in services like a professional resume review, conference attendance, or certification may enhance your prospects. The most important thing to remember is that an intelligent, balanced approach can significantly boost your job search effectiveness.
- **Putting your plans into action**. Now that you have your goals identified, it's time to put them into action. Returning to the premise of marketing yourself as a product, establishing a personal marketing plan that you can act on will serve you well here. Allison Herbert, the product leader, suggests considering your goals and values as a "north star" to ensure that you approach those roles which most closely resemble your values and support goal growth.
- **Remembering to remain adaptable**. As the old saying goes, "no plan survives contact with the enemy". The best strategies are flexible enough to survive the realities of implementation and in the case of job searching, this is true. Rarely is a job search process a linear one. You will need to remain aware of, flexible, and adaptive to changing job markets, financial results, and technology trends.

Operating as a Storyteller

Your Portfolio

One of the biggest differentiators in job-finding success is your ability to tell your story well. For creative careers such as Customer Experience, your portfolio allows you to shine as you highlight successes while you communicate your story. As Madison shared with me, a balance of well-written storytelling and imagery is key to illustrating your story. Your portfolio is different from and should complement your resume by illustrating how you applied those skills to achieve results. A well-crafted portfolio will help you stand out from the crowd through careful selection and creation of the right stories. Done well, you can illustrate your drive, expertise, and approach to solving challenges.

The best way to approach the story is to format your story in the STAR format (the Situation that was happening, the Task you were asked to address, the Action you took, and the Results you achieved) and then add any appropriate visuals to support the story. The description of the Results that were achieved because of your involvement is probably the most important part of your STAR story in any context.

You may be concerned that you don't have enough work history to create a portfolio. Madison informed me that from a recruiter's perspective, portfolios can take a variety of formats including a well formatted PDF, a Dropbox of documents, or well-constructed Google slides that share the story of your impact in STAR format with nice visuals. They don't have to be expansive websites. If you're just starting out, two to three case studies are sufficient.

If you don't have work experience, consider getting involved in volunteer work in your community or church to build some stories and practice your skills. By having a well-constructed portfolio ready to share, you can significantly enhance your job search as a customer experience professional. Remember, it's your chance to shine and make an impression on potential employers.

Your LinkedIn Profile

Your LinkedIn profile is another tool that is important to use as vehicle to tell your story. It is used by over 800 million potential employers, recruiters, and industry professionals. Considering this tool your "front door" to the professional world is an appropriate model to follow. Given this level of potential visibility, you should consider your profile as the resume that an enormous number of potential contacts can see. A well-crafted profile will highlight your skills, experience, accomplishments, and education on a platform that makes your information highly visible. Be sure to use relevant keywords and set your location to the largest nearby metropolitan area to ensure you begin to show up in search results.

Interviewing

The last but probably most important opportunity to tell your story is during interviews. All your prior efforts to land a job hopefully will lead to the interview process and you need to be prepared. Generally, you can expect to go through three or more interviews for a position. In every case, you should plan to exhibit all the attributes below, with questions appropriate for the person who is conducting the interview.

- Clear communication, transmitted through practiced, concise, confident answers to questions using the STAR method.
- Positive attitude.
- Professional dress, even if the interview is virtual.
- Active listening.
- Enthusiasm for the company and role.
- Positive body language such as good posture, maintaining eye contact, and being still, composed, and relaxed.
- Curiosity about the job in the form of thoughtful questions appropriate for the role of the interviewer.
- Gratitude in the form of a follow-up email sent immediately, thanking the interviewer for their time.

Many people worry about the salary conversation, which will likely come up early in the process. The key is to be prepared to answer in an informed way with a range that is accurate for level, role, and geographic area. Within the United States, some states require that employers display salary ranges on job postings. This information doesn't mean that you're eligible for the full range. Organizations set salaries based on the role, level, and geography. Government agency sites such as the Bureau of Labor Statistics may help you to determine where you should possibly estimate where your salary may fall within a given range based on your geographic area and relative cost of living.

Many employers use professionally developed salary databases to set salary levels and pay bands. Salary reports on public sites like Glassdoor or Salary.com shouldn't be considered accurate. You can arrive at your target salary range by reviewing plenty of job descriptions to get a feel for the prevalent numbers. Your more senior contacts, especially those who are hiring managers, may be able to help guide you regarding appropriate salary levels based on your experience and the type and size of the organization.

My recommendation is to let the person interviewing—usually the recruiter—lead the conversation by asking for your expectations. You can provide a well-informed answer because you've done your homework.

Operating as an Evangelist

When job searching, give yourself the best chances at success by being your own best advocate and chief promoter. When you operate as an evangelist, you *want* people to know you're looking for a role, and you want them to know that you're a great candidate who is engaged and informed. Successful evangelists allow their personality and authenticity to shine. They're targeted and specific to ensure that they're spending time on the right activities with people who can most likely connect them to their next roles. Finally, successful evangelists are consistent. It's important to remember that job searching is a marathon, not a sprint, and you should prepare to spend time, energy, and effort over a longer period. A small effort over a longer period will likely provide greater results and self-satisfaction than a big burst of productivity followed by nothing. As Madison advised, treat your job search like a job.

A key task to tackle when you are operating as an evangelist is refining your value proposition and personal branding. To do this successfully, develop, refine, and practice your concise answer to the question, "why should I hire you?" There will be two ways to frame the value pitch that results from this answer. One version will be general, and suitable for any audience. This is the one to use outside of job interviews. The other answer should be used when targeting specific jobs.

When considering your targeted answer, base it on the value you expect to be able to provide to a potential employer. You can gain clues by the job description as well as information about the company available through your network, the company's website, and possibly even news articles or press releases. Connect your answer back to the company's challenges. You may need to reframe the way you answer this question for each company, but you can accomplish this by contextualizing your general pitch to fit the company's needs.

Another way to self-evangelize is to create or refine and expand your online presence. You can do this through LinkedIn optimization, content creation in the form of shared industry-related articles, insights, and updates on professional social media platforms, speaking at local affinity groups, and continuing to refine your portfolio. This allows you to invest back into yourself through expanding your professional point of view and refining your storytelling materials.

You may also get considerable value by participating in networking activities such as industry events, affinity groups, or reconnecting with old colleagues. You may even want to consider requesting informational interviews with your new contacts gained through networking to learn more about their careers and companies. These activities keep you connected and allow you to feel purposeful and engaged during your search.

Conclusion

Ultimately, your search will be unique to you and dependent on the market conditions at the time. Investing in networking, taking a strategic approach to job searching and career development, becoming an excellent storyteller, and being comfortable with self-evangelizing are all skills that will serve you well throughout your career. I wish you the absolute best in finding the perfect role!

From the Editor

Karl Sharicz, Editor

"No author dislikes to be edited as much as s/he dislikes not to be published."

Russell Lynes

Those that know me well enough realize that I am the kind of individual that follows the road less traveled, likes the colors that most others reject, asks the questions that no one else dares to ask, engages in niche hobbies that may not be widely practiced by the majority, and actively chooses to go against societal norms and expectations, whether it's related to relationships, career choices, or personal beliefs. Ultimately, what sets individuals apart is their unique combination of experiences, values, and choices, which shape their paths in life in ways that may differ from the majority.

That's the premise that set the wheels in motion for this book—the follow-on companion to my first book, **CX-PRO: A Practical Guide for the New Customer Experience Manager**. That 2023 publication was authored entirely by me and was based on learnings and skills I developed during my first decade in the field of Customer Experience Management (CXM) that I wanted to share with others entering the CX discipline as a means of grounding them in the fundamentals of CX.

That, along with the **CX-PRO—Training and Certification** training course that I developed and began offering in 2016, reflected the best CX practices that I came to learn, understand, appreciate, and apply over those formative years. Now, with the benefit of my prior twenty years in CXM along with a cadre of supporting authors, I present to you this next book in the series titled, **CX-PRO: Beyond the Basics**—*Advanced Insights for Customer Experience Professionals.*

The authors chosen as contributors for this book are also in an individualistic class of their own. I intentionally tapped into the lesser-known personalities within the field of CX yet those with insights and experiences well beyond their would-be reputation as CX experts and or CX thought leaders. Far too many self-claimed or crowd-labeled CX thought-leaders are little more than CX thought-repeaters, chugging out the same ideas and thoughts of the real CX pioneers before them, perhaps with a new and different label or personal brand.

My aim was to reach beyond the CX echo-chamber and dig deeper into the talents and experiences of those that undoubtedly paid their dues navigating the CX pathway but, for whatever reason, either escaped or intentionally avoided the CX limelight and were not likely to become a contestant in the CX personality game. This, to me, makes them more aligned with some of the real CX pioneers that you may have never heard of but who rose to the challenge of CX long before those two letters and the words Customer Experience were even coined.

The term "customer experience" gained prominence in the business world during the late 1990s and early 2000s. While it's challenging to pinpoint an exact moment or individual responsible for coining the term, its emergence coincides with the increasing focus on customer-centric strategies and the recognition of the importance of delivering positive experiences to customers.

One significant milestone in the development of the concept of customer experience was the publication of "The Experience Economy: Work Is Theater & Every Business a Stage" by B. Joseph Pine II and

James H. Gilmore in 1999. Their book discussed the shift from providing mere goods and services to creating memorable experiences for customers to differentiate businesses and drive success.

Since then, the term "customer experience" has become widely used across various industries, encompassing all interactions and touchpoints between a customer and a brand throughout the customer journey. Organizations increasingly prioritize improving the customer experience to enhance customer satisfaction, loyalty, and ultimately, business success.

Within this book, each chapter has been meticulously curated, authors personally selected by me to represent an expert discourse on various facets of customer experience (CX). Unlike the previous CX-PRO book, where I authored every chapter, here, each author brings forth their profound expertise with a fervor cultivated through their personal journey, manifested in their distinctive style and voice. This anthology invites you to avoid conventional linear reading. Instead, choose any chapter based on your interests and curiosity, allowing it to guide you through the labyrinth of CX insights.

In my role as editor, I've read and evaluated every word, engaging with each contributor to ensure their topic and narrative aligns with the intent of the book. Enclosed within the appendix are the biographies of our esteemed authors, fostering a bridge between reader and author. Their collective efforts have molded this second CX-PRO volume into a seamless continuation of the foundational discourse on CX. Together, both books furnish a dual-volume compendium, catering to the CX community's thirst for knowledge and, particularly, those embarking on the path to becoming respected and successful Customer Experience Professional.

Appendix A—Author Biographies

Jim Bass, CCXP, CX-PRO

Jim is an NPS Certified Customer Experience and Engagement Strategist located in Alpharetta, GA. His 20+ years' experience designing CX at key moments of truth and critical touchpoints along the customer journey map comes from 14 years at McKesson Corporation where he led customer support and advocacy, 5 years at ADP where he managed survey operations and insight analysis for National Accounts, 1 year at Macquarium where he was CX design consultant, and 1 year at Verizon Connect where he managed their VOC program and implemented text analytics.

During his tenure at these companies, he envisioned, implemented, and led many proactive programs, projects and initiatives designed to increase customer satisfaction, engagement, and loyalty while containing/reducing costs and minimizing churn.

His CX perspective is that improving customer experience does not always have to be a daunting or expensive venture. Businesses can improve revenues and profitability by making a few simple changes in behavior, communication, listening and, most of all, acting. Jim is also a published songwriter and genealogist.

Judy Bloch, CCXP

Judy Bloch is an innovative Customer Experience leader with a passion for process improvement, driving change, and designing connected omni-channel experiences. She has created quantifiable CX results in leadership roles at multiple Fortune 50 brands and has won various industry awards and nominations throughout her career including CXPA Innovation Award (2017), Texas Tech Titans (2017) and North American Customer Centricity Awards (2021). Currently she serves in a consulting role, working with global brands to deepen their CX programs. Judy currently serves on the Kansas State Industrial Engineering Advisory Board, as well as the Missouri State University CX Program Advisory Board previously.

Eckhart Boehme, Founder & Managing Director, unipro solutions GmbH & Co. KG

Eckhart Boehme is a seasoned professional with a diploma in industrial engineering and over three decades of diverse experience in marketing, product management, and skills development on a global scale. With a career spanning more than 30 years, Eckhart has honed his expertise through various roles and responsibilities, contributing significantly to the advancement of industries and organizations.

Eckhart's journey in the professional realm has been marked by a remarkable tenure of over 18 years at Microsoft Corporation. During his tenure, he held pivotal positions in product management, marketing, and marketing education. His strategic insights, innovative approaches, and dedication to excellence played a pivotal role in shaping the direction and success of numerous initiatives within the technology giant.

Throughout his career, Eckhart has demonstrated a relentless commitment to driving growth, fostering talent, and spearheading transformative projects. His deep understanding of market dynamics, coupled with his passion for continuous learning and development, has positioned him as a trusted leader and advisor in the field.

Beyond his corporate endeavors, Eckhart is known for his dedication to mentoring and empowering aspiring professionals. He is actively involved in sharing his knowledge and experiences through various channels, including speaking engagements, workshops, and industry forums.

Eckhart's journey serves as a testament to the power of expertise, resilience, and visionary leadership in navigating the complexities of today's business landscape. With a track record of accomplishments and a relentless pursuit of excellence, he continues to inspire and impact the next generation of leaders in the field.

Mark Borst

Mark has served over 30 years as a workplace consultant in the corporate furniture industry, collaborating with design professionals to support new ways of working. In the last decade, Mark's focus pivoted to client experience strategy, where he engaged design-thinking methodologies and the art of inquiry to uncover client aspirations and foster client-centricity in organizations.

As a Customer Experience Designer, he developed robust and comprehensive initiatives to drive cultural transformation through customer-centricity. As a Workplace Consultant he has collaborated with designers and architects, transforming space to help people work, heal, and learn better.

Mark is a dynamic, creative, and results-oriented leader with a record of successfully engaging with designers, customer experience professionals, and organizational teams to ensure an elevated customer experience. He is hands-on professional, passionate about strategic change, and especially knowledgeable in theology, polity and contemporary challenges facing churches and non-profits.

Mark is comfortable with creating thought leadership content, moderating workshops, public speaking, and leading engagements with leaders, employees, congregations, and customers. Mark is a certified Pine and Gilmore Experience Economy Expert (#116) and is also CX-PRO certified. Most recently, Mark created Rekklessia, a consultancy which helps churches and non-profits explore fresh futures.

Alec N. Dalton, CHT, CCXP

Alec Dalton, A passion for five-star service fuels Alec Dalton's leadership in customer experience and quality management. His background ranges from operating five luxury hotels to holding various corporate positions with industry leaders like The Ritz-Carlton Hotel Company and The Walt Disney Company.

Alec conducts research and teaches via a courtesy appointment to the faculty of Florida International University's Chaplin School of Hospitality and Tourism Management. As the Executive Director of Accelerating Leaders, he provides management consulting partnership across the service industries. Additionally, Alec serves on the boards of HorizonCX and the Customer Institute, judges several international customer-centric awards, and is a frequently sought speaker on CX, quality strategy, and hospitality management.

The International Hospitality Institute has ranked Alec among the "100 Most Inspirational People in Global Hospitality & Travel." He co-authored the first two books in the best-selling series Customer Experience, as well as the textbook Operations Management in the Hospitality Industry. Ultimately, Alec enjoys helping brand-names and boutique businesses, non-profits, and governments set new standards for service excellence.

Gary C. David, PhD, CCS, Professor of Sociology and Experience Design, Bentley University

Gary is a Professor of Sociology and Experience Design at Bentley University. As a Certified Clinical Sociologist, he is interested in using social science as a foundation for helping clients design solutions to achieve their goals and overcome barriers. He has worked with a variety of companies on improving experiences for customers, employees, patients, learners, and users. He also is co-host and producer of Experience by Design podcast, where they "explore experience designs of all kinds." He has spoken to international audiences about the importance of belonging and connection as part of experience design, focusing on the power of coming together to elevate our experiences.

Rich Dorfman, CX-PRO, Director, Customer Experience Strategy, Eastern Bank

Since introducing the customer experience role at Eastern Bank in 2008, Rich has managed and evolved CX at the company to where this strategic initiative is deemed a corporate imperative in sustaining a differentiated, competitive advantage. His role encompasses the breadth and depth of the CX discipline: program design & delivery, VOC measurement & financial linkage, insight analysis & reporting, governance & strategy, and principle CX advocate & transformationalist.

He tirelessly engages with frontline colleagues, business line leaders and executive management to leverage the voice of the customer in a way that drives both better customer and employee experiences, and importantly, the desired business performance outcomes. Rich's relentless pursuit of leveraging essential outside in, customer-centric perspectives into everyday decision-making has helped Eastern sharpen its focus on and alignment around the customer while supporting the company's brand promise, "we do good things to help people prosper."

In addition to his day job at Eastern, Rich is a leader within the Boston CXPA network, a sought-after speaker and panelist at CX conferences, and soon to be an adjunct professor of the first-ever graduate degree program in Customer Experience Management at Michigan State University teaching qualitative research methods.

Scott Gilbey, EMBA, B.Sc., P.Eng., CCXP

Scott is a self-prescribed "Experience Handyman," taking a handyperson approach to the field of experience, bridging the gap between strategic objectives and frontline realities. In business generally, there has been a persistent and decades-long gap between what executives say they deliver and what customers say they expect and receive. There is no shortage of strategy, vision, or leadership, and still, CX metrics waver. Scott does not claim to have "the" answer. He certainly has "an" answer. It's at the frontline.

Scott's career began as a Professional Engineer in Canada, with school paid through jobs in hospitality as black-tie waiter, bartender, and cruise ship deckhand. He later fed his family with roles in manufacturing operations, sales, marketing, and general management. His responsibilities grew, including post-acquisition mergers, safety, ISO certification, master data and GDPR data privacy, culminating in Customer Experience on a global scale based in the U.S.

In his near-retirement years, out of sheer curiosity, Scott returned to the Frontline in a rotating series of hourly Frontline roles, getting into the weeds on customer service, cashier vs. self-checkout, BOPIS (buy online pickup in store), airline member status, and more. Scott has become a CX provocateur and budding author.

Laurie Gray, Sr. Director, User Experience & Design, CBORD

Laurie is a seasoned UX/CX leader and product manager with over 20 years of experience. Her expertise spans user research, product strategy, and design, with a proven track record of building and mentoring high-performing teams. Laurie's gift lies in solving communication breakdowns between groups that others find difficult to solve, such as breakdowns between brands and customers or technology and users.

She is currently Senior Director of UX and Design at CBORD, where she and her team are actively improving the user experience of food service and access control management software for users in healthcare and higher education settings.

In her free time, she is active in motorsports competitions including track-based events in her vintage Austin Healey Sprite. She's also a state-certified beekeeper, and a wife and mom.

Marc Mandel, CCXP

Marc is a certified customer experience professional who's enjoyed a nearly thirty-year career helping companies to think differently about their customers and employees. Over the years he's been a consultant, executive coach, and more recently, provider of advanced voice-of-the-customer analytics systems.

There are few things he enjoys more than seeing companies truly transform and become true champions for their customers. Some of Marc's best clients include the largest insurance companies, banks, healthcare providers, media, retail, and technology companies in the Fortune 1000.

Marc and his wife Lisa and their three Cavalier King Charles Spaniel dogs live in Wake Forest, North Carolina. As a family and when not collaborating with clients, they enjoy their beloved Durham Bulls minor league baseball, visiting the white sand beaches of the North Carolina Outer Banks, and exploring the majestic beauty of the US National Park system.

Alex Mead

Alex Mead is a UK National, globally mobile, currently based out of the Middle East. He specializes in identifying performance improvements across Customer Contact, Customer Service, Customer Experience & Customer Operations. His primary areas of concentration are contact center modernization, digital transformation, customer experience innovation, CRM implementation and design, operations improvement, and introducing AI solutions that benefit customer and employee journeys.

With more than 25 years of global CX and Contact Centre experience, Alex has been voted Global CX Thought Leader by Frost & Sullivan and several of the companies he has worked with have been recognized with Industry awards for the Customer Transformation initiatives he has led.

Mr. Mead is highly adept at identifying inefficiencies with the way companies operate their global contact centers and customer service, analyzing customer experience issues and operational failures, putting forward clear plans for operational improvements. He works across people, processes, and technology, and has an incredibly detailed understanding of the global outsourcing frameworks and benefits that can be provided through BPO.

Alex has spent over 25 years leading global Call Centre & Customer Experience with large global brands including IAG, Rentokil Initial, Barclays Bank & Edrington, as well as high-growth start-ups operating within Travel, FinTech & Banking sectors. In these roles he has delivered significant transformations, achieving Industry Award winning CX recognition whilst also reducing OPEX by up to 40%, at the same time improving customer experience, advocacy, and retention measures by over 25%.

Greg Melia, CAE, CEO at CXPA

Greg has served as the CEO of the Customer Experience Professionals Association since April 2019. His previous experience includes frontline service, organizational development consulting, and 17 years developing and supporting nonprofit professionals in their career development.

He holds a graduate certificate in Creative Problem-Solving and Change Leadership from the International Center for Studies in Creativity, the Certified Association Executive professional certification from the American Society of Association Executives, and degrees from The College of William & Mary and The London School of Economics. He lives in Columbia, SC.

Ken Peterson, President—CX, QuestionPro

Ken has over a quarter century in helping customers succeed through customer experience research across retail, technology, hospitality, financial services, automotive and transportation industries. His expertise includes financially linking business outcomes, SaaS deployments, and CX consultation and has worked with every major SaaS Customer Experience platform provider. With a background in Mathematical Operations Research, he's eager to find ways that companies can be more profitable through taking actions from customer feedback.

Ken has also had the privilege of helping clients to improve their customer engagement in travel, sports, and media to better understand how to make use of the vast quantities of data that is now available, but often underutilized and misinterpreted. Delivering relevant insights, fact-based execution, and bottom-line results which has led to multiple publications and 2 US CXA Awards in 2022. His work is frequently published by industry trade publications.

Jerry Seufert

Jerry is a consultant, executive coach, and small groups facilitator based in Alpharetta, Georgia, along with being a resource to CXPA local networks and CX practitioners. Jerry is an accomplished customer experience visionary, executive counselor, product advisor, change management expert, critical thinker, writer, and facilitator. As a small group moderator, coach, advisor, and organizer of multiple CX community groups, Jerry has been part of thousands of conversations with CX professionals from all walks of the community at differing stages of their working lives around the globe.

Jerry's 'first home' was in the health industries where he led more than 100 projects for hospitals, health systems, provider groups, federal and state health agencies, and solutions vendors, and now serves clients across several product and service sectors and individuals at all stages of their professional journeys. Jerry has a B.S., Biology, and M.S., Industrial Engineering, from Rensselaer Polytechnic Institute.

Karl Sharicz, EdM, CX-PRO

Karl brings over thirty years of skills and experiences gained in high-tech research and manufacturing B2B environments along with proven business acumen. Throughout his career, he has served in a broad range of roles within marketing, sales, training, and training management—developing internal and external customer relationship skills and building a decided customer-centric focus along the way.

In his former corporate role within Tyco SimplexGrinnell, a leading fire and life-safety provider doing business throughout North America, Karl served as Customer Experience Lead where and his team focused on driving those elements of the customer relationship and experience that increased customer satisfaction, reduced customer churn, and increased customer lifetime value.

Karl is steeped in the Customer Experience Management discipline, including developing customer-centric cultures; determining the voice of the customer and deriving insights and understanding; fostering organizational adoption and accountability; creating customer experience strategies, designing approaches that will achieve customer experience excellence, and setting up metrics and measurement systems that help drive organizational return on investment.

Through his knowledge of adult education and learning styles plus prior experiences as a director of training, he offers additional skills in developing structured learning environments. During his tenure at Tyco for example, Karl developed the Next Improvement in Customer Experience (NICE) Workshop concept that has been in operation throughout the organization since 2010 and driving new levels of customer focus leading to increased customer retention. He has developed certification programs for professional services teams and was a certified consultative sales trainer and coach.

Karl is a United States Air Force veteran and served during the Vietnam era. He holds a master's degree in education from Boston University, is actively engaged with the Customer Experience Professionals Association (CXPA), initiated, and led the CXPA Boston Network and event planning committee. Karl also formerly served on the original CXPA Board of Directors for five years as well as having served on several other key CXPA committees. He also served in past leadership positions within the American Society for Training and Development (ASTD). In addition to his professional CX persona, Karl doubles as a singer-songwriter and musician and has recorded two CDs of his original music.

Mark Slatin, CCXP

Mark is a CX thought leader, consultant, coach, and faculty member, and podcast host. Recognized as one of the Top 25 CX Leaders Globally by CX Magazine, Mark's dedication to enhancing human experiences is more than a profession; it's a personal mission. He created The Trusted Guide Roadmap™ Master Class, a next level course, designed to provide CX leaders with proven frameworks and practical tools to get executive buy-in.

Mark's tenure as a Professor of Practice at Michigan State University underscores his profound influence in shaping the next generation of CX professionals within the inaugural Master of Science in Customer Experience Management (CXM) program in North America.

Prior to founding EmpoweredCX, Mark launched and led an award-winning CX practice at Sandy Spring Bank. During that time, the Bank received numerous awards including The CX Innovation Award, Great Places to Work, Forbes America's Best Bank, and American Banker Best Bank to Work For, and The Washington Post Top Workplace.

Mark is a Certified Customer Experience Professional (CCXP), recently served on the CXPA Board of Directors and he's also the creator and host of The Delighted Customers Podcast, which consistently ranks in the top 10 of Apple Podcasts in Management. Beyond his professional endeavors, Mark finds fulfillment in family moments, community projects, and the occasional round of golf.

Patty Soltis, CCXP, CX-PRO

With over three decades of experience, Patty has led numerous organizations through change management to profitability using the CX discipline. She is currently a senior customer experience manager at Upwork. Patty was a principal analyst—CX for eMarketer/Insider Intelligence and a patient experience consultant for Moffitt Cancer Center. She was a consultant for several years working with both small and enterprise organizations and served as a VP/GM for Neiman Marcus, Marshall Fields, and Lord & Taylor.

Patty is a CCXP, CX-PRO and was named a CX Influencer by CX Network in 2024 and CX Scoop in 2023. She is an active member of the CXPA as a leader on the FL network and on the Regional Council. She is a member of HorizonCX Board of Advisors and supports the Michigan State University CXM program as a speaker and advocate.

Patty is a proud graduate of the Indiana University Kelley School of Business and earned her MBA from Oakland University. She has several certifications from Florida Atlantic University and the University of South Florida including Value Creation, Post Crisis Leadership Management, Diversity, Equity, and Inclusion and more.

www.ingramcontent.com/pod-product-compliance
Lightning Source LLC
Chambersburg PA
CBHW041811110726
48006CB00019B/2341